Anonymous

Statistics and Information Concerning the State of Missouri and Its Cheap Farming Lands,

the grazing and dairy region, and limitless opportunities for labor and capital. With compliments of the General passenger department of the Missouri Pacific. Vol. 1

Anonymous

Statistics and Information Concerning the State of Missouri and Its Cheap Farming Lands,
the grazing and dairy region, and limitless opportunities for labor and capital. With compliments of the General passenger department of the Missouri Pacific. Vol. 1

ISBN/EAN: 9783337298586

Printed in Europe, USA, Canada, Australia, Japan

Cover: Foto ©ninafisch / pixelio.de

More available books at **www.hansebooks.com**

STATISTICS AND INFORMATION

CONCERNING THE

STATE OF MISSOURI

AND ITS

Cheap Farming Lands,

The Grazing and Dairy Region,

The Mineral and Timber Resources.

The Unsurpassed Fruit Lands,

AND

Limitless Opportunities

for Labor and Capital.

WITH COMPLIMENTS OF THE

General Passenger Department

OF

The Missouri Pacific Railway Co

⇢MISSOURI.⇠

LOCATION.

MISSOURI, on account of its central location, is destined for a commanding position in the sisterhood of States. The geographical position of a State or country has as great a bearing on the importance of that State or country financially, politically and socially as all other influences combined. Why is New York the Empire State? Why is its influence felt so strongly in all matters of national importance? Why do the sister States look to New York to lead? Why are the political and financial policies of the country dictated from New York? While the United States was confined to the region east of the Allegheny mountains, and the commerce of the country west was of no importance, Virginia, on account of its central location, exerted the controlling influence in the affairs of the nation. Her soil was superior to that of New York, her climate was more genial, and her natural adaptation to acquiring wealth in all branches of industry surpassed that of New York. Her statesmen and great men were made greater because they were citizens of Virginia, and their influence was augmented by the proud position of the great State which they represented. But how great the change. Virginia has lost nothing. In fact, her gain in spite of a disastrous war, has been steady. But how is it with New York? When the Star of Empire was pushed over the barriers of the Alleghany mountains, and the army of emigration took possession of the rich farming lands in the Mississippi valley, the streams of commerce and humanity commenced to flow east and west, instead of north and south. New York harbor was the central point toward which these streams converged, and New York, on account of her commanding position by the sea, held the world for tribute, going and coming, and grew in wealth and power as the nation extended westward. Thus it is seen that New York held its position, not by virtue of its natural fertility or mineral wealth, but because of its location relative to the other States.

New York will doubtless always maintain her supremacy, but there are influences at work that will build up a rival in the West. In a country so large as ours there must necessarily be interests which are more or less antagonistic while in no way interfering with the stability of government. The West being an agricultural region, exclusively, finds itself out of harmony both in the matter of finance and political economy with the East, which is largely manufacturing. The center of population, wealth and power has been steadily moving westward since the beginning of the century, and the tendency has been to seek a permanent lodgment in the Mississippi valley. Every advance westward and the admission of every new State has lessened the influence of New York and the East on the affairs of the West and has forced it to a greater reliance on its own resources and the principles that should govern their development. Then, too, the North and the South have not wholly recovered from the antagonisms of the war. But the South is developing its natural resources at a wonderful pace. The Southwest has increased its population 60 per cent in the past eight years, and over 5,000,000 of people have been added to the population of the whole South since the census of 1880, and the increase in wealth both in manufactures and agriculture has been even more rapid and phenomenal. The interests of the South and West are identical and the reconciliation of the whole country lies in the harmonious working together of those two sections, for their common good. Therefore nothing is plainer than that the West must have a common center where its own commercial, political and social interests will crystalize; but there must also be a common ground on which to meet the South and East. There is no State that has so even an adjustment of forces as Missouri. Here are found in about equal proportions representatives from the North and South, the East and West. The methods, ideas and sentiments of all sections here work harmoniously together. They understand and respect each others principles.

St. Louis is rapidly becoming the commercial center of the Mississippi valley. It overshadows the whole Southwestern trade, and gives its protecting influence to every line of production and traffic. In St. Louis then questions concerning the welfare of the whole country can be equitably and impartially adjudicated and it will exert an influence, independent of its commercial greatness, that will be felt in the remotest

MISSISSIPPI RIVER BELOW ST. LOUIS. IRON MOUNTAIN ROUTE.

corner of the United States. Missouri will change from a State of local to a State of national importance, and the citizen, the merchant, the professional man, and the congressman, will have added to his own abilities and influence. the weight of his citizenship of the great State of Missouri.

MISSOURI.

As is well known, the State of Missouri is **situated** geographically almost in the exact center of the United States, and is also the central State of the Mississippi valley, and is about equi-distant from the Atlantic and Pacific oceans, east and west and Canada and the Gulf of Mexico, north and south. Its area is 69,415 square miles or 44,425,600 acres, the greater portion of which is tillable. Its physical features are varied unique and wonderful. But after all, the most striking feature of this great State, is the decided abandonment with which Nature has lavished her choicest gifts. No region in the world has received equal recognition at her hands. On mountain and in vale, on hill and plain, there flourishes in superabundance, every article that can be absorbed by man in the progress of civilization. Emerald pasture lands, where thousands of cattle graze and get themselves in a sacrificial condition to supply the hordes of humanity sweeping westward with food, where mobile flocks supply the golden fleece for man's apparel, where staple grains that feed the world spring from the prolific soil at the waving of labor's wand.

Sturdy mountains hold within their metal sides rich deposits of iron, lead, and numerous other minerals that meet the wants of civilization and add to the wealth of the State. The hillsides teem with vineyards, and grapes as luscious as were ever ripened by the sun of Burgundy or Rhineland are compressed into sparkling wine. And where does earth reveal a region with a more abundant variety of vegetation and more prolific of its fruits and flowers. Vast forests, the growth of centuries, deepen the shadows of the landscape and whose depths furnish the timber that is fashioned by the skillful hand of the artisan into a thousand shapes and forms of usefulness and beauty. Throughout the State are inexhaustible deposits of lead, zinc, tin, iron, kaolin and granite. A combination of fertile prairie and waving forest, green pasture and limpid stream, make a delightsome landscape to be seen in its perfection nowhere else.

And this is the country we would tell you of. This is the country, as it shall be shown, where Nature has been more lavish in the bestowal of elements of wealth and happiness, prosperity and great and inexhaustible wealth than anywhere else in the world. Missouri is a State that luckily has escaped the blighting influence of the boomer. While she has been fortunate in this respect, she has perhaps been retarded in development by the too conservative spirit heretofore displayed by her citizens and by a lack of judicious and legitimate advertising. The people of Missouri now see the necessity of making the resources and advantages of the State known to the world, or get left far in the rear in the rush of civilization and the development of the Southwest. The country to the west and southwest has been so much more clamorously advertised than Missouri, that the latter State has been in a measure overshadowed, and it is not known that in its borders are rich farming, grazing and fruit lands, which can be purchased at not much greater cost than the unimproved lands of the far West; and unlike them, they have the advantages of schools, society, railroads, markets and many other similar benefits which are denied to the first generation on the virgin soil.

It has long been a matter commented upon by persons familiar with Western emigration, that home-seekers pass through the State of Missouri and on to the extreme frontiers of Kansas and Nebraska—paying for land in sparsely inhabited neighborhoods, prices, in some instances, greater than those charged for better lands over which they have passed to reach the wilderness. There can be found within the State of Missouri farming lands as fine as the sun ever shone on, which are held at prices as low as prevail two and three hundred miles farther west. And yet of the immense stream of immigration that annually pours westward, but a very small proportion halts until it reaches the very borders of civilization. This is caused by the fact that persons who leave the populous East to seek homes and cheap lands in the West, set out on their journey under the impression that in the thickly settled portions of the Western States prices are very much higher than on the frontiers. The result is that without any investigation whatever, they go on and on until they reach the end of the railroads, or at least the remotest settlements, and arriving there by the thousands, find the competition of purchasers far greater than prevails in a portion of the country through which they have journeyed. Hence they pay larger prices for land remote from the markets, in neighborhoods enjoying none of the benefits pertaining to a thickly populated region, and are compelled to labor for years at a disadvantage they could have avoided by settling in the older portions of the States through which they have passed.

The mistake of Eastern people who come West to buy farming lands is that they leave home in charge of a land agent, and never look to the right or left until they find themselves near the foot-hills of the Rocky Mountains. Here they invest in "wild prairie" that never has been, and probably never will be reliably productive. Meanwhile they pass through the most fertile agricultural region on the continent, where land is offered at very low rates, and on reasonable terms, where failure of crops is almost unknown, where markets are convenient and agriculture profitable. If you are about to remove to the West, beware of excursions into the wilderness.

Missouri comprises a portion of the garden spot of the West. There cannot be found on the continent an area of country equaling it in fertility and natural resources, nor one more happily situated with reference to the great markets of the country. The actual value of land ought to bear a relation to the convenience of its locality to markets as well as to its qualities in other respects. Therefore land within reach by rail or otherwise of the Missouri river points should be far more valuable than lands more distant, for Missouri river points are and will be for all time to come, the markets in which the products of a large portion of the State must be sold. It will pay persons seeking Western homes to tarry a while in Missouri before buying land. Having done so, they cannot fail to come to the conclusion that there may be such a thing as going a little too far west just for the sake of getting a chance to grow up with the country. In this portion of the great West, enterprise has taken a strong, fresh, new hold, and the New South and the New West are growing together. The vast resources are bringing hither every branch of manufacture, and the time is not far distant when along the banks of the "Big Muddy" the great manufacturing centers of the world will exist. Only a little while ago this region imported its canned vegetables from the Atlantic coast and its canned fruit from the Pacific. To-day, because of the fact that on one acre of Missouri bottom land more of such vegetables can be raised than on double that amount of Eastern land, and because our orchards can be made as prolific as those of California, the trade of both the East and West in both classes of goods mentioned, has rapidly fallen off and the Missouri valley has become self-supporting in that particular. Moreover, the land which is so much better is far more plentiful and very much cheaper, and in a little while the Missouri valley, already an exporter, will be furnishing the world with canned fruit and vegetables.

In thousands of other directions among the comforts, necessaries and luxuries of life, the Missouri valley region will become the supply depot. Our fields of grain, flocks and herds of sheep, cattle and swine, mines of iron, lead and zinc, quarries of stone, beds of sand and hundreds of inexhaustible resources have already brought hither planing and flouring mills, furniture factories, starch factories, breweries and distilleries, meat packeries, weaving establishments, foundries and many other like enterprises, and they will be doubled and redoubled many and many times, and to them will be added hundreds of other lines of art and manufacture, gathering material for their product on the ground.

The teeming East should and will learn of this, and that there is room and employment for countless thousands in this vast region, openings for investment where energy and enterprise will prove the talismanic keys to fortune. To this fair and fertile section a hospitable people invite the industrious from everywhere.

The bona fide homeseeker, the capitalist and investor are wanted in Missouri and to them the State will be a revelation. You will not find here an El Dorado, dollars cannot be found as thick as autumn leaves in Valambrosia, nor can wealth and happiness be acquired without the sweat of honest toil. But you will find a land where industry receives its sure and rich reward, and judicious investments will bring an abundant increase. Your life and property will not be hazarded by the blizzards that sweep the North, nor your grains and grasses be shriveled by the hot winds of the sun-parched deserts of the distant West. You can at moderate cost locate yourself on some of as fine land as the sun ever shone on right along the great highways of commerce between the East and West, where the arteries of traffic are throbbing with ever increasing activity. Here is a country right in the midst of civilization where a small investment aided by intelligent labor will bring its sure reward of wealth, where churches and schools, culture and enlightenment, hold undisputed sway over a peaceful people.

PHYSICAL FEATURES AND SOIL.

MISSOURI is situated in the geographical center of the Republic, in the Mississippi Valley, having that river sweeping its eastern boundary, with the Missouri separating it nearly in the center, flowing east and west, and from Kansas City northward, forming its western boundary. Nature's means of transportation are abundantly provided. The waters of these two rivers afford a cheap and convenient means of carrying on commerce between the principal cities of the State and of bordering States, and also an outlet for the products of the western part of the State to the East, and brings it in water connection with Memphis, New Orleans and the gulf and ocean. Thus, without railroads Missouri would be by no means helpless and cut off from the commerce of the outer world. Upper Missouri may all be included in the Mississippi, Missouri and Grand river valleys, and is nearly all prairie, the timber being confined to the narrow stretches that skirt the streams principally. The prairie land is, for the most part, high and rolling, except the river bottoms in the immediate vicinity of the rivers, and the soil of the whole of northern Missouri is deep, rich and easily cultivated. Even indifferent cultivation brings abundant harvests. South of the Missouri river, except in the extreme west, is the timbered and broken part of the State. The southwest section referred to is similar to north Missouri and contains, at present, nearly all the desirable farming land of the State, that may be had at low rates and to which it is especially desired to invite the attention of those looking for good, cheap homes. The remainder of the country south of the river, while not so well adapted, as a whole, to general farming, contains the mineral and timber wealth of the State, and, in addition, some excellent farming lands in the river bottoms, and it nearly all affords grazing that can be surpassed nowhere. This comprises the Ozark region of the State and is, consequently, more broken than the northern part; and, to the southwest of St. Louis, toward the southern boundary of the State, the hills attain the height and dignity of mountains, many rearing their abrupt granite peaks among the clouds.

The scenery here is all picturesque, some of it attaining the grand and sublime. While not possessing so rich a soil as the northern part of the

State, Nature has bestowed her wealth in a different form. Here are found the rich iron, lead, zinc and kaolin mines of the State. And here is dug the coal that supplies the Western world with fuel. It is idle to speculate upon the extent of the mineral deposits beneath the surface of the State of Missouri. It is a question that many ages in the future will not be able to solve, no matter how vast exploration and removal may draw upon its stores. The Iron mountain is the largest exposure and the purest mass of iron known on the earth. Missouri, without doubt, now produces more lead than all the States combined, and zinc is quite as abundant.

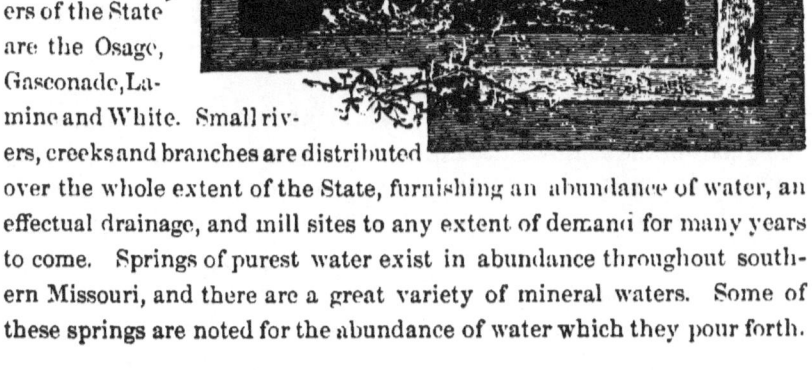

The other navigable rivers of the State are the Osage, Gasconade, Lamine and White. Small rivers, creeks and branches are distributed over the whole extent of the State, furnishing an abundance of water, an effectual drainage, and mill sites to any extent of demand for many years to come. Springs of purest water exist in abundance throughout southern Missouri, and there are a great variety of mineral waters. Some of these springs are noted for the abundance of water which they pour forth.

The soils are of great variety, as is shown by the State Geologist's report, and are adapted to the production of all kinds of grain, fruits and vegetables in their greatest perfection, known to the temperate zone. Timber varies with the soil and embraces a very wide range of the choicest varieties of both hard and soft woods. Among the most valuable timber found are the sweet, black and yellow gum, the pine, beech and tulip tree. The hard wood varieties are oak, walnut and hickory, elm, maple, ash and locust, cherry, cottonwood, pecan, box elder and chestnut.

The geological sub-stratum is, to a great extent, carboniferous—vast areas of coal hidden beneath the surface, sufficient to furnish fuel that might warm the continent for untold ages, and plainly designating Missouri for the great manufacturing State of the Union in the years to come.

Turning now to the soils of Missouri, we find every variety, both prairie and timber, and of every conceivable depth above the geological formation. These soils are indicated, in a state of nature, as well by the growth of grasses upon the surface of the prairie as the growth of trees in the timbered regions indicates the quality of the soil which nourishes their roots. One of the finest bodies of prairie land in the world can be found in the chain of counties extending along the Missouri river from Callaway all the way to Atchison. The drainage of this country in the main is excellent. The soil is rich, quick and productive. The prairies yield abundantly of corn and the smaller grains, and constitute the finest meadow lands in the world. The alluvial soils of the rivers are composed chiefly of sand, lime and vegetable mould, and their wonderful fertility is generally considered indestructible. These alluvial soils are generally devoted to the cultivation of corn, hemp, tobacco, Irish potatoes and hay. Wheat upon the virgin soil grows too luxuriantly and is liable to tumble or lodge, and no attempts should be made to grow the latter grain until several years of other crops.

Another soil of great productiveness is found in the northwest counties and a part of the southwest counties of the State. It is usually of gently rolling prairie and is underlaid by the upper and middle coal measures. The agricultural products are corn, wheat, hay, oats, barley, potatoes, and in fact almost any products of the State. As a consequence, cattle, hogs, mules, horses and sheep flourish here. This soil is black from the presence of lime in quantity, and if the lime-stone contains iron, the soil is red or brown, but its productiveness is not thereby lost. Another distinct class of soils is found South of this region, and on a belt extending from the Arkansas line to the Missouri river. This class has a reddish clay soil, is a fine corn and wheat country and admirably adapted to fruit and sheep culture. This soil is based on magnesian lime-stone and abounds in fine springs and very heavy timber.

The last class of soils is that on lands elevated higher than other portions of the State, being from 1,200 to 1,500 feet above sea level. It is underlaid by sand-stone and magnesian lime-stone. Black oak, hickory, pine and cedar flourish here, and the grape is grown in perfection. In its valleys and on some of its slopes the lands are very fertile, and yet in compensation for a less generous soil, Nature has given to this region a deposit in mines of mineral and metal that can stand the drain of the world's wants for hundreds of centuries.

CAMP SCENE.

The location of Missouri for all agricultural purposes is the most desirable that could be found. Being in the geographical center of the United States, north and south, neither extreme of temperature is ever experienced. Howling blizzards and temperatures that run the mercury twenty, thirty and forty degrees below zero are as utter strangers to the State of Missouri as the scorching heat and fiery sun of the South. Then, too, the seasons of seed time and harvest are long. The farmer has ample time to get his ground in condition for the planting. The crop has a long season to mature and corn is never in danger of the early frosts of autumn. The winters are short and there are very few days that the farmer cannot be employed in outdoor pursuits. This is an advantage, too, that must not be overlooked in the economy of raising sheep and cattle. The winter is short and the profits of the farm are not consumed in carrying the stock through till spring. Stock can nearly make a living from the range, and, unless it is desired to fit them for the market, very little feeding is required. The range of farm produce raised in Missouri is exceeded nowhere. There are all the grains and vegetables of the

North in the greatest perfection, the great staples, wheat and corn, making the highest average per acre. All kinds of fruits reach their highest perfection here. In the raising of apples and pears Missouri is already a formidable rival of the East, and when all of her orchards come into full bearing, this State can control the Western market. The wonderful results already reached in this branch of agricultural industry are surprising when its comparative infancy is taken into consideration. In the raising of small fruits, Missouri has exceptional advantages, for, in addition to reaching their greatest perfection here, both in quality and quantity, the early seasons enable the producers to put them on the markets of the country in advance of the glut which annually occurs, thereby securing the highest prices. They are also in position to supply the late and exhausted markets of the South.

CATHEDRAL SPIRES ON THE MERAMEC. LINE OF MISSOURI PACIFIC RAILWAY.

When all these advantages are taken into consideration, and, in addition, the comparative cheapness of rich, improved lands in desirable communities, with every advantage of society, schools and churches, no candid and fair-minded person will deny the superiority of the claims of Missouri on the consideration of the intelligent farmer who is seeking a home in the great West.

Another division might be made into prairie lands and timber lands. Each division contains soils of all grades of productiveness.

Bisecting the State by a line drawn from the city of Hannibal, on the Mississippi river, to its southwest corner, the half lying to the north and west of this line may be described as the prairie region of the State. That which lies east and south of the bisecting line is the timbered or forest section, in which are found numerous prairies of greater or less extent. The prairie lands are again divided into bottoms and uplands. The bottom prairies closely resemble in soil the river bottoms. In a certain sense the formation is identical; each came from accretions—one from the rivers, and the other from the higher or upland prairies. The marl formation is the foundation of both, and in both it is deeply buried under the modern alluvium. They owe their extraordinary fertility and inexhaustible productiveness to a borrowed wealth, which came to them in endless supply from the loosened soils of the higher lands by means of overflow and abundant rains. The river bottoms are generally bounded by timber or bluff lands; occasionally they extend, by gentle swells, into prairie bottoms, which occupy a higher level, and are often grand and sublime in their vast extent. Undulating or rolling like waves in their endless succession, the upland prairies often appear as limitless as the sea, and present the appearance of the ocean when subsiding from the effects of a storm. Also they are the sources of enormous wealth, and are objects of never-failing interest and attraction to the agriculturist, who well knows with what ease they are cultivated, and how gratefully they reward his labor. The bottoms of the rivers and streams are distributed over every portion of the State, and are similar in formation and soil to those of the great rivers. In this book it is not necessary to give minutely the classification of the soils of Missouri. A general survey of the field is all that the farmer will require.

The hackberry lands are first in fertility and productiveness. On these lands also grow elm, honey locust, hickory, white, black, burr and chestnut oaks, black and white walnut, linden, ash, poplar, catalpa and maple. The prairie soils of about the same quality are known as crowfoot lands, so-called from a species of weed found upon them, and these two soils generally join each other where the timber and prairie soils meet. Both rest upon a bed of firm silicious marls, and even under most exhaustive tillage will prove perpetually fertile. On this soil white oaks have been found twenty-nine feet in circumference and one hundred feet high, linden twenty-three feet in circumference and quite as lofty. The burr oak and sycamore grow still larger. Prairie grasses, on the crow-foot lands, grow very rank and tall, and by the old settlers were said to entirely conceal herds of cattle from view.

The elm lands are scarcely inferior to the hackberry lands and possess nearly the same growth of timber. The soil has about the same properties, except that the sand is finer and the clay more abundant. The same quality of soil appears in the prairie known as the resin-weed lands.

Next in order are hickory lands, with a growth of white and shellbark hickory, black laurel and scarlet oak, sugar maple and persimmon. In some portions of the State the tulip tree, beech and black gum grow on lands of the same quality. Large bodies of prairie in the northeast and southwest have soils of the same quality called mullatto soils. These hickory lands, and those mentioned as similar to them are highly esteemed by farmers for the culture of corn, wheat and other cereals. They are also admirably adapted to the cultivation of fruits and their blue grass pastures are the equal of any in the State.

The magnesian limestone soils extend from Callaway county south to the Arkansas line and from Jefferson west to Polk county, which can be traced on the county and sectional map in the back of this pamphlet. These soils are dark, warm, light and very productive. They produce black and white walnut, black gum and elms, sugar maples, chestnut, black post, laurel, scarlet and Spanish oak. They are among the most productive soils of the State and yield fine crops of all the staples. Thrifty fruit trees and vines evince their adaptation and fitness for the production of all kinds of fruits in an extraordinary degree. Large, bold springs, of limpid, pure and cool water, gush from every hillside and flow away in bright streams, giving beauty and attraction to the magnificent forests of elm, oak, mulberry and buckeye which often adorn their borders. The mining regions embraced in this division of the soils, are thus supplied with vast agricultural wealth and a large mining, pastoral and agricultural population may here be brought together in relations scarcely to be found in any other country of the world. Bluegrass and other succulent and nutritious grasses grow luxuriantly, even on the ridges and hillsides of the upland forests, in almost every portion of southern Missouri. Located in the midst of a temperate and charming climate, with its fountains and streams, its valleys and elevated lands will attract and delight sooner or later vast populations. On the ridges where the lighter materials of the soils have been washed away or where originally wanting, white oak lands are to be found, the oaks accompanied by shellbark and black hickory, and trees and shrubs of smaller growth; while the surface soil is not so rich as the hickory lands, the subsoil is quite as good, and the land may be greatly improved by turning the subsoil to the surface. These produce superior wheat, good corn, and a very fine quality of tobacco. On these lands fruits are abundant and a sure crop.

Pine lands are extensive and embrace a large area of the southern portion of the State. The yellow pine, which constitutes largely the growth of this district, grows to a great size and furnishes immense supplies of marketable lumber. They are accompanied by heavy growths of oak which take the country as successors to the pine. The soil is sandy and well adapted to small grains and grasses.

The tillable soil of Missouri especially adapted to cultivation and to the most varied agriculture is of great variety and excellence. Its rare ingredients are rarely found in the same combination elsewhere. In the most hilly and broken portions of the State are rich valleys; those unfit for cultivation are covered with valuable timber. About 2,000,000 acres of government lands remain still undisposed of, and while the best of these lands have been culled, small and very valuable tracts may be entered under the homestead and pre-emption laws. The railroad companies still own large quantities of land.

In every county in the State farms and improved lands can be purchased at very low prices.

CLIMATE AND HEALTH.

EVERY other advantage being equal, the climate will turn the scale for or against a country and determine the land seeker in his choice of a home. It is intimately connected with the well-being of its inhabitants, and is indeed the most essential element of this well-being which nature can grant them. So that then the consideration of the climatic condi-

18   MISSOURI.

tions becomes of the first importance in the selection of a country which is to become the permanent home of our families. Missouri lies almost in the center of the North American continent, It is therefore essentially an inland State, with all the advantages and disadvantages of such an inland, or as it is termed scientifically, a continental climate. Two rivers, the largest on the continent, the Mississippi on the eastern border, and the Missouri through the center of the State, and their numerous affluents, favorably modify the climatic conditions. Its elevation above the ocean varies from 300 to 400 feet in the southeastern portion of the State to 1,200 and 1,600 in the southwest.

ON BIG RIVER.   A REMINISCENCE OF THE PAST.

The State is situated just on the limits of the wooded portion of the Mississippi valley and of the western prairie country, and partakes of both conditions. The watershed of the Ozark mountains passing through the southern portion of the State, from northeast to southwest, attain a maximum elevation above the surrounding country of 800 feet, but are not high enough to exert a perceptible influence on the climate.

The mean annual temperature is about 55 degrees. The mean winter temperature is 33 degrees and of summer 76 degrees. While in winter the temperature sometimes gets below zero, and in summer up among the highest figures at the top of the thermometer, these extremes are of but short duration, not lasting long enough to occasion any inconvenience or discomfort in either direction. The winter as a whole is moderate and mild, with very little snow, and no long storm-locked periods when it is with difficulty that the farmer can keep up communication with dwelling and stables, and much less with the outside world. On the contrary, cattle require very little stabling and only a moderate amount of feeding in comparison with the amount of care necessary on a Northern farm. The summers are no hotter than in the more northern States. The heated periods are of longer duration, perhaps, but are the source of very little inconvenience, and no loss to the farmer, like the long winters of the North.

Another element of a desirable climate for agricultural purposes, to be taken into consideration, is the amount of rainfall and its distribution throughout the different seasons. The average annual rainfall for the State is about 41 inches. It is the least in winter and highest in summer. This is a high average, but insures the absence of extensive droughts, which bring such widespread injury in some parts of the country. And notwithstanding this large amount of rainfall, the climate is a dry one, for the most abundant rains fall in a very short space of time, and clear skies is the rule, and cloudy, overcast heavens the exception, especially in the summer and autumn. The universal reign of sunshine is a condition of the climate which is of the greatest importance for the well-being of the inhabitants. In summer and autumn there is rarely a day without some sunshine, and in the other seasons rarely three days pass without some break in the clouds. A continuation of a week's gloomy weather is a great rarity, even in the darkest months. All of which is conducive in a great measure to the happiness and well-being of humanity. The south and southwest winds are the prevailing ones, especially in the warmer seasons, and in the winter west and northwest are equally as prevalent. Winds usually prevail at all seasons, rendering the greatest heat of summer tolerable, but rarely reaching the dimensions of tornadoes, which are so frequent farther west.

The natural as well as the cultivated products of the soil attest the favorable influences of the climate on organized life. From the largest timber down to the smallest and least significant members of the vegetable kingdom the greatest perfection of growth is attained.

The climate of Missouri is on the whole very favorable to the prosperity of the human race, and a great and happy community will enjoy the benefits a bounteous nature has so generously lavished upon the entire State.

In conclusion, it is especially desirable to call the attention of the farmer who is desirous of obtaining a home in the West to the advantages to the agricultural industry of the mild, short winters which prevail in the State of Missouri. The advantages of mild, open, short winters are not fully appreciated by the farmer in changing from a colder to a warmer State. A short, open winter gives him the opportunity of working nearly every day in the year, and not hibernating for five or six months, as the farmer of the North is compelled to do. It saves hired labor, giving him a much longer season for doing his work. It saves him great expense in carrying his stock through the long winter, to say nothing of the great saving in fuel, clothing, health, etc. He can keep his farm in better condition and culture, and that with his own labor, than if he were restricted to a shorter season. These advantages are more than the farmer can estimate, and the amount saved in a year in the milder climate would represent a fair profit on a moderate sized farm. The money saved is the money made on a farm, as well as elsewhere, and farmers who contemplate a change would do well to look into the merits of a short winter season in its bearings on farm economy.

The conditions on which general healthfulness depends, are exceedingly favorable in Missouri. The climate, as we have seen above, is the most desirable to be found in which to live throughout the entire year. The summers are not extremely hot, nor the winters extremely cold, and there are consequently none of the dangers to life and health which attend the opposite conditions. The atmosphere may be called a dry one, notwithstanding there is abundance of rainfall. There is very little gloomy, overcast weather when the sun is not seen for days at a time; when rains occur, they fall fast and copiously and are followed by a clear sky and bright sunshine, which quickly clears the atmosphere and earth of lingering moisture, that otherwise remaining would brew the germs of sickness and general unhealthfulness. The altitude and rolling surface of the State is also favorable to good health. Only a small portion of the State can be designated as swampy. The remainder is of a character which would be called decidedly broken or rolling. In some sections the hills rise to the dignity of mountains, and at no point in the State is there a lack of diversity of surface sufficient to hold in check any amount of rainfall and prevent the most thorough drainage consistent with the best sanitary conditions.

The home seeker may know, that in making Missouri his home, he is not coming in a State where he will endanger the most priceless possession of himself and family, their health, but on the contrary, he may be assured that the chances are vastly in favor of a decided improvement, not only pecuniarily, but also in the conditions of health.

We have then to sum up, a soil of the highest grade of natural fertility, abundance of rainfall to produce the greatest results in all kinds of grains and fruits, a climate unsurpassed, and the other conditions of health almost perfect. Now we are to see how all these natural conditions are being utilized. What are the present conditions of agriculture and the opportunities offered to the home seeker and the future outlook of this industry in Missouri.

AGRICULTURE.

ITS PRESENT AND FUTURE.

MISSOURI is essentially an agricultural State. The present status of this industry, however brilliant of itself, is but a promise of the future While ranking among the foremost States in the production of the staple cereals as to amount and value, it is comparatively a new agricultural State, with a large amount of land that has never been brought under cultivation, and a still greater quantity which is only made to yield an iota of what it is capable, owing to its cheapness, the large tracts in which it is held, and the lack of improved methods and systematic culture, such as are characteristic of the older and more thickly populated East.

In 1889 the population of Missouri was 2,568,380 of all ages. Of this number 792,959 were engaged in the various occupations, whereby men can make an honest living and support those dependent upon them. Of

GRAND CANYON, SULPHUR SPRINGS, ON THE MERAMEC. MISSOURI PACIFIC R'Y.

this latter number, 375,297 were engaged in agricultural pursuits, and making their living from the soil of the State of Missouri. Nearly half were thus engaged as against those of all other occupations. Thus it is seen that agriculture outstrips any other industry and indeed preponderates over them all combined in regard to the number of inhabitants engaged in them.

These 375,297 people produced in 1889, of the leading cereals as follows: corn, 213,500,000 bushels, or more than the total product of the whole United States in 1860, making her third in the yield of corn.

Wheat, 23,350,000 bushels, and eighth in the yield of this staple.

Oats, 38,666,000 bushels, standing sixth in this cereal.

Rye, 535,426 bushels, again standing eighth.

The value of the potato crop of the same year was $4,689,694.

The milk products were valued at $4,173,017.

The butter yield was worth to the farmers $33,572,124.

These are a long way from being the entire agricultural products of the State. No figures are here given for the stock industry, sheep and wool growing, the large quantities of fruit, including the immense business done in grapes and wine growing, and various other smaller products which bring millions into the pockets of the farmers annually.

The above products were raised on 29,177,990 acres of land, which has an assessed valuation of $395,633,307. These figures show conclusively that Missouri ranks among the first great agricultural States of the Union. It is in the lead in the leading products of the soil. It is the geographical center of the Mississippi valley, the geographical center of the United States, and of the North American continent. It is in direct communication by water with the ocean and the commercial centers of the world. It is the center of the commerce of the great Mississippi valley and is in direct communication with the Atlantic seaboard by means of all the east and west through railway lines. It is central in point of latitude, thus avoiding the long cold winters of the North, as well as the dry hot summers of the South. It affords a great diversity of pursuits to the tiller of the soil—greater than almost any other State. All the cereals are grown in the greatest perfection and yield the greatest returns. All the fruits, grains and vegetables of the North as well as those indigenous to the South attain the greatest perfection in Missouri. The wheat grown in Missouri makes the best flour and is eagerly sought in European markets. If properly sown in fair soil the yield ought to be in an average year, thirty bushels per acre, and indeed many farmers often obtain that yield on their entire crop. The Eastern farmer with his improved methods could even increase this large yield. Corn nowhere attains greater perfection than here, and the soil and climate are perfectly adapted to growing all kinds of fruits. Large areas of the finest pasture lands are found in different parts of the State, and stock, sheep and wool growing are by no means the least of her industries.

The preceding may serve to give a brief idea of the agricultural interest of the State of Missouri. But these are figures of a State only partially developed, and are just a suggestion of what may be accomplished when all her agricultural resources have been developed and made to approximate their greatest perfection under prevailing conditions.

There are vast agricultural opportunities still undeveloped in Missouri. There is still a large opening for the farmer who is intelligent, industrious and economical.

The State of Missouri contains 42,625,600 acres all told. Of this there are still unimproved 14,480,610 acres. This is of course not all adapted to agricultural purposes, much of it being mountainous and broken to such an extent as to make it available, at its best, only for grazing purposes. Some of it is covered with a dense growth of valuable timber. But a large quantity of this area is excellent farming land and as productive as any in the State. In addition to this there is considerable land in southeast Missouri still owned by the St. Louis, Iron Mountain and Southern Railway which is of excellent quality for general farming, and may be purchased at low rates for cash, or may be obtained on time payments on easy terms and long extension of time.

But the greatest inducements to home seekers lie not so much in the unimproved lands of the State, as in the low prices of the semi-cultivated and improved lands to be found in all parts of the State and in some of the most favorable localities. There is no State having such excellent soils, superior railroad facilities, close proximity to markets and with all the advantages of schools and social privileges where farms are so cheap as in Missouri. For years the stream of western immigration has passed through Missouri to the so-called cheap lands of the West, where they paid nearly as much for the bare prairie without a stick of timber or a board set up on the end to keep off the howling winds or shelter them from the blizzards. They have been contented to live for years in a dugout, when, with no greater cost in the long run, they might have been the possessors of improved farms with snug homes, where their families might live in comfort, within a short distance of ready markets, with good schools for their children and churches where they might worship with their families and accumulate a compentence for their old age without undergoing the discomforts of a home in the wilderness.

Missouri offers no lands to the settler for pre-emption. The chief inducement, as we have said before, is the cheap, improved, rich farming lands of the State. On account of large holdings and unimproved methods of farming, the State's capacity for production has by no means reached its limit. There is no reason why Missouri should not produce double her present harvests of all crops and become the leading agricultural State of the Union. In size, point of location, fertility of soil, proximity to consuming centers, transportation facilities, climate, etc., it has all the promises of a glorious future. A man with moderate means can come here and buy a good farm with all the advantages enumerated for no more than it would cost to prove up on a government claim in the West and erect suitable buildings for his family and stock.

To the home seekers of the Eastern States and to the traveler from across the seas, Missouri has been a comparatively unknown land and an unfamiliar name, while widespread advertisements have made other less favored sections, with their attractions, real and assumed, household words in immigration centers. For years these facts have been commented upon and the apathy of Missourians relative to immigration criticized. But this is a thing of the past, and now through the efforts of a number of public spirited men, Missouri is to be advertised as she has never been before, and the quickening into new life that is now beginning to be felt through all the avenues of trade, through the efforts of these enterprising gentlemen, is to be pushed to the very flood tide of prosperity and activity that will place Missouri in the position she is entitled to by virtue of the advantages with which nature has endowed her.

PRODUCTS

ALL grains, fruits and vegetables do well in Missouri. A greater number of the foregoing products reach perfection within the limits of this State than any other similar area that the whole world could boast.

WHEAT.

Wheat culture here cannot be excelled. The land is rolling, well drained and dry. The climate is all that could be desired and the crop rarely suffers from the effects of the severe winters and deep freezing of the more northern latitudes which are frequently so fatal to this cereal. The yield is uniform—varying but slightly from year to year—increasing with the increase of acreage. Missouri ranks among the leading wheat States.

The following table gives the amount of wheat in bushels in eight of the leading grain producing States of the west for 1887, and shows that Missouri stands well up in the lead in the production of this cereal:

Michigan,	21,672,000
Indiana,	37,828,000
Illinois,	36,861,000
Wisconsin,	13,063,000
Minnesota,	36,299,000
Iowa,	26,837,000
MISSOURI,	**27,744,000**
Nebraska,	16,585,000

It will be seen from the above that Missouri is fourth among the wheat producing States of the Mississippi valley in total quantity of wheat produced. The table below shows the average per acre of the same States for the year 1887:

Michigan,	13 bushels per acre.
Indiana,	13 " "
Illinois,	15 " "
Wisconsin,	10 " "
Minnesota,	11 " "
Iowa,	10 " "
MISSOURI,	**16** " "
Nebraska,	10 " "

MISSOURI.

The last table is the best test of the adaptability of a State to wheat growing, and in the yield per acre for the whole State, Missouri is clearly in the lead with the high average of 16 bushels per acre. The only State of the group approaching her is Illinois with 15 bushels per acre. The inference must be drawn from this, that Missouri, in fertility of soil and adaptability of both soil and climate to wheat growing, takes first rank among the States in the production of the great food staple.

The tables following may be useful, and while they show that on account of distance from the seaboard, Missouri farmers did not receive as much per bushel for their wheat, they more than made up the difference in the greater yield per acre and the superior quality of the grain :

Michigan,	$10 per acre.
Indiana,	10 "
Illinois,	10 "
Wisconsin,	4 "
Minnesota,	7 "
Iowa,	7 "
MISSOURI,	**10** "
Nebraska,	5 "

Table showing the total value of the wheat crop of the eight leading wheat States for the year 1887 :

Michigan,	$16,037,000
Indiana,	27,236,000
Illinois,	25,802,000
Wisconsin,	8,360,000
Minnesota,	21,416,000
Iowa,	16,370,000
MISSOURI,	**17,201,000**
Nebraska,	8,790,000

The wheat raised in Missouri is of the best milling quality and is much sought after both at home and in foreign markets. We think there is not much need for further explanation, as the foregoing figures speak for themselves more eloquently than words can. There is a vast quantity of splendid wheat land still unturned that can be made as productive as that already under cultivation, awaiting the enterprise of the immigrant.

CORN.

Indian corn or maize is the leading agricultural staple of this country. It has usurped the throne of cotton as king of American products. The total corn-yield of the United States for the year 1887 was 1,456,161,000 bushels, having a market value of $646,106,770.

This is not the largest yield ever known. It has been surpassed frequently. But owing to the high prices prevailing in 1887, it is the greatest market value ever placed on this crop or any other at any time in the history of the United States. Of this amount, Missouri produced 140,080,000 bushels, and the farmers of the State pocketed $52,151,000 as their share of the profits of this crop. In no State is Indian corn more at home, and it is one of the most profitable crops to the farmer. Its yield depends largely upon the soil upon which it is grown and the character of the cultivation given to it. On ordinary soil, with careful cultivation, it should yield from forty to fifty bushels per acre. As a matter of fact, however, the average yield is much less than this for the whole State, as will be seen in the following tables. Corn was a light crop throughout

ON CURRENT RIVER, MISSOURI.

the whole corn belt last year, and the average was small, but there is no reason why the yield of corn for the State of Missouri should not be doubled without increasing the area planted by a single acre. Farmers on good lands, who take extra care of their corn, can obtain a return of eighty bushels per acre easily. It will bring cash always, as the farmers of Missouri are near to good markets, and it is the cheapest and best feed with which to fatten his pork, beef and mutton, which are always in demand at the best prices. It is a crop easily raised, suffers little from droughts, unless greatly prolonged, and cannot be injured by rains after it is ripened and before it is secured. In fact, the farmer can take his own time in harvesting, gathering it at any time during the winter, when other work is not pressing, thus avoiding the heavy expense of harvesting other crops.

Below is given a table of the corn crop raised in the eight leading corn States for the year 1887:

Iowa,	183,502,000
Illinois,	141,080,000
MISSOURI,	**140,949,000**
Nebraska,	93,150,000
Kansas,	76,547,000
Texas,	76,490,000
Tennessee,	75,204,000
Ohio,	73,797,000

As in the production of wheat, Missouri is among the leading States, but in the raising of corn is nearer the head of the list, being the third, and only a few thousand bushels behind Illinois, which is second in the list.

The following table gives the value of the corn crop of the same States for the same year, with Missouri in the third position:

Iowa,	$64,225,700
Illinois,	57,842,800
MISSOURI	**52,151,130**
Nebraska,	27,945,000
Kansas,	28,322,300
Texas,	39,009,900
Tennessee,	37,602,000
Ohio,	35,422,000

Average yield per acre of same States:

Iowa,	25 bushels per acre.
Illinois,	19 " " "
MISSOURI,	**22** " " "
Nebraska,	24 " " "
Kansas,	14 " " "
Texas,	17 " " "
Tennessee,	21 " " "
Ohio,	26 " " "

In the average yield per acre, Missouri comes into fourth place; but not because of inferiority of soil or other natural conditions. With a vastly inferior soil, New York State produces thirty-three bushels per acre of corn, or eleven more than Missouri. Rocky and barren little Maine, with a scanty, miserly soil, gives an average of thirty-five bushels to the acre. With the same cultivation and treatment Missouri ought, with her superior soils, at least to double her present average per acre. Besides, 2,000,000 acres might be added to the area devoted to this crop without making a proportionately greater amount than is planted in Iowa and Illinois yearly. This additional acreage could be planted without encroaching upon the area devoted to any other crop.

Wheat and corn are the principal grain productions of Missouri; the most money is made from these crops and consequently more attention is given to their cultivation than to the others. Oats, rye, barley, buckwheat, etc., thrive here and reach great perfection both in the quantity produced and the quality of the crop. Oats can be sown early and give immense yields and they always find a ready market. The annual production is about 25,000,000 bushels, not very much of which goes East, but is shipped to the South and Southwest, where there is always a demand for this class of grain, and Missouri is happily in a position to supply it. The other cereals mentioned are not much grown owing to the greater profit there is to the farmer in the staples of corn and wheat.

GRASSES AND PASTURAGE.

The next most valuable agricultural product to corn in this country is hay. The annual value of the hay crop of the country is between 350,000,000 and 400,000,000 dollars. It has been truly said that grass lays the foundation for all successful agriculture. In a State where grain growing is carried on exclusively, the soil, no matter how deep and fertile, soon deteriorates and loses its fertility in a greater or less degree, as the course of events has clearly proven in some of the foremost agricultural States. But where grain, grass growing and cattle raising are carried on simultaneously, and in a well balanced proportion, the soil retains its fertility and brings a double profit to the farmer in the shape of butter, cheese and fat cattle in addition to grain, and prevents the exhaustion of the soil.

There are few or no grasses that are peculiar to Missouri, and it is fortunate it is so, for were it otherwise, it would argue some peculiarity in the soil or climate that would perhaps, unfit them for many varieties of this great and almost universally diffused family of plants. The country that has a limestone soil can raise all kinds of grasses and has the basis of all agricultural prosperity. Everywhere grass grows luxuriantly and all known varieties thrive equally well, and nature having provided the wild grasses so bountifully, the cultivated grasses have, until recently, been neglected. The soil and climate make this State the natural home of all the nutritious grasses and is particularly adapted to the famous blue grass which is so celebrated for the production of the high grade and priced stock of Kentucky. This springs up spontaneously wherever the soil is left free from the plow and pasture. Many instances of this kind could be cited showing how kindly this invaluable grass takes to the soil, furnishing when not grazed during the summer a most invaluable winter pasturage, and productive here, as in Kentucky, of the same fine horses and cattle, and bringing the same high prices in the market. Other varieties of grasses are fully its equal for pasturage and have the additional advantage of being cut and cured for hay. Farmers should sow a variety of grasses to secure a constant and regular supply of food for their stock. Orchard grass, timothy, red top, millet, Hungarian grass, alfalfa and clover take kindly to the soil, and in recent years have been extensively grown for pasturage and hay, and the latter for soiling and enriching the soil. Men who wish to raise stock are advised by some to go farther west and engage in the business on a large scale, but they should remember that the best parts of the range are occupied and fenced in, while at the best it is a hazardous business. One summer of extreme drought, or a winter of unusual severity, may blast all their hopes. Not so with Missouri. It is bounded and traversed by mighty rivers and their tributaries, and it is not subject to the terrible droughts which occur on the Western plains; should a severe winter come there is always plenty of hay and cheap forage in this great grain-producing State.

STOCK RAISING AND DAIRYING.

AMONG the industries that go to make Missouri a great State, stock raising is by no means the least. Without disparaging or underrating other States, it can be truthfully said that for stock raising, Missouri possesses unsurpassed advantages and all the conditions which go to make a successful stock-raising State.

Undulating land is the coveted home for stock. They will not do so well on low level lands. In Missouri there are hills as rough as the highlands of Scotland, extensive valleys fertile as those of the Nile, and prairies interspersed with beautiful groves of timber.

CORN HUSKING, MISSOURI.

Missouri reveals the spectacle of a State containing the finest grazing land right in the midst of a fertile and productive farming country, and surrounded by the most celebrated cattle markets in the country.

Long experience and careful estimates of the cost of land, and the amount and cost of forage necessary to raise and fatten the different kinds of stock for market justify the positive assertion that horses, cattle and hogs can be raised and fattened for one half of what it costs to do the same in the Eastern and Middle States, while sheep can be raised for one-third. There is no State so advantageously located with respect to good markets and nearness to consuming centers, and having at the same time such cheap and fertile lands, and where the cost of raising, fattening and getting them to market is less than right here in Missouri. The surface, the soil, and the climate of the State are such as to be conducive to the health of all farm animals. Contagious diseases, so common in some States, do not infect the flocks and herds of Missouri.

The shipping facilities in all directions are unsurpassed, both by water and rail. The great trunk lines of railroad cross the State east, west, north and south, putting all sections in direct communication with the seaboard and great interior markets.

To the southwest of St. Louis there is a region well watered, well timbered and shaded, clothed with nutritious grasses, where cattle can be herded and driven gradually southward to winter in the cane-brakes of Arkansas, and in spring to return upon the growing grass, until they are in one day's journey of their market; or where shelter can be easily and cheaply supplied, and crops raised in the valleys cheaply bought for feeding cattle during the winter if that should be desired; where supplies are quickly and cheaply reached; where there is no triangular fight between settlers, cattle and sheep men; where herders would be welcomed as buyers of stock and crops, and where their early lambs and calves could be cheaply and quickly marketed.

The success of dairying in Missouri has been fully tested. Natural yellow butter of the very best quality is made throughout the year. A prominent and intelligent butter dealer and dairyman, who has had fifteen years experience in New York and twenty years in Missouri, expresses the decided opinion that this, as a dairy country, surpasses that of New York, Ohio or Wisconsin. He thinks the climate more favorable, the grasses better and the easy butter making period much longer, while the support of stock costs much less. North Missouri is washed by innumerable rivulets, creeks and small rivers, with rapid currents. The timber and prairie lands are in about equal quantities. This whole country is undulating and a soil of extra fertility. The streams never go dry. The winters are short and snow rarely covers the ground for one continuous week and the climate is healthful for man and beast and unusually favorable for the increase of the latter, and has all conditions necessary to the greatest results in the dairying interest. Milk, butter and cheese, can as a consequence be produced cheaper and with less labor in Missouri than perhaps anywhere else. What has been said of North Missouri, is applicable to the greater part of that portion of the State lying south of the Missouri river. Much of this section of the State is quite broken and the extensive Ozark formation may be called mountainous. It is generally more thinly settled and much of it is the finest pastoral region on the globe. The streams are more numerous than in northern Missouri, and the water in this mountainous region, cooler and more unfailing, and the remarkable springs of Pulaski, Newton, Franklin and other counties, furnish a wonderful supply of cold water of uniform temperature throughout the year. Cattle uniformly graze until Christmas, and the crop of nutritious milk producing grass that springs underneath and is protected by the blue grass, if permitted to grow in the fall, affords excellent winter pasturage.

This country, while possessing all the natural advantages of New York, as a successful dairy region, is quite as well situated as to markets for these products as the Empire State, as the great metropolis of the Mississippi valley, St. Louis, is on the east and Kansas City, St. Joseph and numerous smaller cities in the interior are on the west, and it is well connected by through railway lines with the great Southwest and Rocky Mountain region, where very little dairying is carried on. The market for this class of products will be constantly enlarging, which will create an increasing demand, which will only be limited by the resources of the State in this direction. The shipping facilities are unsurpassed and all parts of the State are in direct and rapid communication with the great population centers and the region of the Southwest and West.

WOOL GROWING.

AS a State for successful wool growing, Missouri needs no long array of fine spun arguments drawn from the fertile imagination of theorists. The business has unobtrusively interwoven itself into the growth and progress of the State to such an extent that its general history could not be perfectly written without recording the growth and progress of wool growing and wool manufacturing within her borders.

A large majority of Missouri farms are of rolling and undulating surface; the soil being rich and productive, both in grains and grasses, making them peculiarly adapted to the business; and no agricultural pursuit, as such, or which may include with it the keeping of any or all other kinds of stock, has been so profitable within the last ten years as has sheep farming properly managed and persistently adhered to.

On the ranch system, chiefly in the counties of southern Missouri, sheep raising has proved very remunerative, and there has been a greater or more certain increase, from the fact that the storms are less frequent and less destructive than in most other pastoral regions. The protection afforded by the mountains or high ridges and hills, on which are generally more or less timber, goes far to give stability and to assure profits to the business.

Their security is not only assured in this way, but also by artificial shelter and protection which may be secured cheaply by lumber from her own timber, abundant in the regions of the State that are so well adapted to a sheep pastoral pursuit. Grain and hay may be provided in all parts of the State for an extended or extraordinary winter.

The sheep do not have to travel miles for their daily supply of water, but springs and streams of pure running water are numerous and abundant.

Another prominent and advantageous feature is the amount of grass which is growing among the timber, in the valleys, on the slopes and on the high hills or mountainous regions of southern Missouri. The grasses are not so tall and coarse as to be unhealthy for sheep, but they are the finer grasses, growing upon lands that are naturally well drained. The

UPPER WHITE RIVER, OZARK MOUNTAINS. IRON MOUNTAIN ROUTE.

climate is mild in winter, especially in the south half of the State. Snows are not frequent, nor do they lie upon the ground long enough to prevent sheep from having a living on the blue grass pastures, which exist, or may easily be secured, in all sections of this State.

Blue grass is indigenous in Missouri. When the timber is removed it springs up spontaneously on the land, and when the prairie is reclaimed it soon takes possession and supersedes all other grasses. This famous grass is the foundation on which the mighty stock industry of Kentucky has been built, and has given a world-renowned reputation to its fine blood horses, cattle and sheep.

There are tens of thousands of acres of land as well set in blue grass as those on which these careful experiments have been made and capable of being handled in the same way by sheepmen, which can be bought now at from ten to twenty-five dollars per acre, and hundreds of thousands of acres upon which blue grass is fast taking hold, and which will eventually be as good, if pastured by sheep, that can be bought for less than five dollars per acre. Facts concerning the value and capabilities of blue grass lands, warrant the assertion that ten thousand acres of these cheap lands, managed as a pastoral sheep ranch, and when fully set in blue grass, will keep more sheep and produce more wool than any ten thousand acre sheep ranch in the world.

The rich and finely cultivated higher priced lands in all parts of the State are well adapted to the thoroughbred flocks of all varieties for the purpose of breeding. Nowhere will the animals of a given breed attain larger size or more fully develop the animal or mutton qualities than in this State. Her thoroughbred sheep will rank with any in the United States, or in the world, and her corn and fine blue grass will produce the best heavy mutton and lustre combing wool.

But the great open domain of Missouri—the counties South of the Missouri River—is that which will interest wool growers who handle sheep on the pastoral plan.

Here large tracts of land may be acquired for not over five dollars per acre, admirably adapted to this industry, on which whole communities of wool growers may settle with their families, and enjoy the benefits of advanced civilization, without exposure to hardships, privations and dangers of border life.

MINES AND MINERALS.

THAT country or State where manufactures and agriculture are carried on simultaneously and in about equal proportions, will be the most prosperous and have the most equitable distribution of wealth. In a State that is exclusively one or the other, the wealth will be found in the possession of certain classes and the inhabitants may be divided into rich and poor. The working of mines and the consequent manufactures brings to a State a large number of inhabitants, who are consumers of agricultural products, and a State that is adapted to agricultural purposes as well as manufactures and mining, will always obtain right in its home markets, the highest prices for farm, garden and dairy products.

We have shown in previous chapters that Missouri was adapted by nature to the most successful cultivation of all farm products, and we have also shown its exceptional advantages as a dairying State. We will now consider its mining and mineral resources and in the evenly balanced condition of these industries, the most casual observer cannot fail to see foreshadowed the future greatness, from a commercial standpoint, of the State of Missouri.

Missouri has an abundant deposit of all the minerals used in the leading manufactures and is well adapted by the presence of extensive and inexhaustible coal fields, for the converting of the raw material, dug from the ground, into the shapes and forms for commercial use.

COAL.

The Missouri coal fields underlie an area of about 26,000 square miles. The southern outcrop of the coal measures has been traced from the mouth of the Des Moines through the counties of Clark, Lewis, Shelby, Monroe, Audrain, Boone, Cooper, Pettis, Henry, St. Clair, Bates, Vernon and Barton, into the Indian territory, and every county northwest of this line is known to contain more or less coal. Outside of the coal fields given above, coal rocks exist in Ralls, Montgomery, Warren, St. Charles, Callaway and St. Louis counties, and local or outlying deposits of bituminous and cannel coal are found in Moniteau, Cole, Morgan, Crawford, Lincoln and Callaway counties. Estimates have been made as to the amount of coal in these deposits; but it is quite unnecessary to give them in this connection, as the reader can readily see that the supply is more than ample for the use of many generations to come.

The coal mines of Missouri are usually easily worked and require no deep shafts or expensive machinery for hoisting or drainage. They underlie the greater portion of the finest agricultural sections, not only of the State, but of as productive a region as is on the continent. Coal of good quality can be purchased at the mines so cheaply, that even when farmers have timber in abundance near at hand, they prefer to burn coal rather than cut and haul wood a short distance. The coal area covers considerably more than one-half of the State, and active and systematic mining has opened the beds in more than a thousand places along the railroads and near the towns. There need never be any fear of a scarcity of fuel in Missouri, and the condition of the farmer here may, in this respect, be considered blessed far above that of those located in many portions of the Northwest and farther west, where buffalo chips, cornstalks and twisted hay are all they can afford to temper the cold of more rigorous winters than we ever experience here.

IRON.

The fame of the iron deposits of Missouri is too well established to require more than a comment upon the bearing this most important metal is destined to have in influencing the future prosperity of the State. A distinguished mining engineer, after giving a detailed account of the mines which have been examined, sums up by saying: "They have enough ore in Missouri to run one hundred furnaces for one thousand years. More could not be desired, without the appearance of too much solicitude for posterity, who would be too far removed to appreciate our good wishes." Iron Mountain, Pilot Knob, Shepherd Mountain, Simmons' Mountain, and thousands of other deposits of lesser distinction, will glut the forges for all time to come of a district yet destined to be one of the grandest workshops of the world. Concentrated in a limited area, surrounded on all sides by the grandest agricultural district of the globe, with unlimited supplies of coal, with timber and water power unsurpassed upon the continent, with a genial climate and healthy homes for the operatives, and their food cheaply produced almost at their doors, with the world for a market, and transportation facilities for reaching its most distant point, it is not difficult to see a most prosperous future for a section so happily situated and so richly endowed.

The manufacture of iron, and the industries growing out of it, are now in the State second only in importance to that of agriculture; and yet these industries are only in their infancy. Hundreds of thousands of tons of ore are shipped out of the State annually, mostly to Pittsburg, Pennsylvania, to be converted into steel and metallic iron, and much of it returned into and across the State in rails and bars and manufactured articles, simply because our mills and manufacturers are unable to supply the demand.

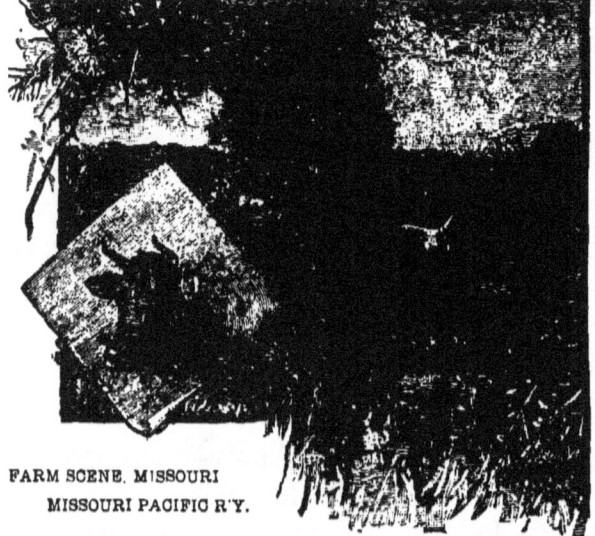

FARM SCENE, MISSOURI
MISSOURI PACIFIC R'Y.

Opportunities for the profitable investment of capital exist in hundreds of industries, ranging from the conversion of the ore into iron and steel to the manufacture of these materials into their most valuable forms. St. Louis, now the third manufacturing city in the Union, and other well located cities and towns throughout the State, are only just beginning to develop the possibilities of their importance as manufacturing centers, and, as they increase, the value of the agricultural lands will be wonderfully enhanced.

LEAD.

Next to iron the most important metal of Missouri is lead. Lead mining has been carried on here for more than one hundred years, and the first discoveries of lead were made as early as 1720. Up to the present time new discoveries have been frequent, and it is now conceded that there is probably no country on the globe so rich in lead deposits as Missouri. The mineral occurs in lodes, veins and disseminations, which are yet only partially determined; but enough knowledge of the extent, depth and thickness of deposits has been acquired to show that their range and richness exceed any other known lead-bearing region in the world.

There are several lead districts in the State, all south of the Missouri river, where the magnesian limestone rock—the great lead-bearing rock of the world—exists. The lead is not, however, strictly confined to this rock, but is also found in a disseminated form in ferruginous clays, slates and in gravel beds, or in cherty masses in the clays associated with the same.

The southeastern lead district embraces all or parts of Jefferson, Washington, Franklin, Crawford, Iron, St. Francois, St. Genevieve, Madison, Wayne, Reynolds and Carter counties, with some mines in the western portion of Cape Girardeau county. Mining has been longest carried on in this district, and the aggregate of the production has been very great. But, with the exception of a few mines, the work has been chiefly surface mining, often carried on by farmers during the winter season, and the great deposits which require capital to develop may be said to have, as yet, been scarcely touched. This surface mining has often been so very profitable that mining lands acquired a great speculative value—too great for their purchase for agriculture—and this has rather retarded the development of this region than otherwise. With the low price of lead which has prevailed for the past three or four years, the lands have again fallen, and the farmer can now buy them below their agricultural value, and, as has often been done, sometimes buy with them a fortune in an undiscovered mine.

The central lead district comprises, as far as known, the counties of Cole, Cooper, Moniteau, Morgan, Miller, Benton, Maries, Camden and Osage. Much of the mining done here, again, has been near the surface, the lead first being found in clays, in caves and in masses in clay but a few inches below the surface. Shafts, however, sunk in the magnesian limestone, find rich deposits in lodes and pockets.

The southern lead district comprises the counties of Pulaski, Laclede, Texas, Wright, Webster, Douglass, Ozark and Christian. It has been but little developed, but it is generally thought that it will prove a profitable field for miners when railways make it more easily accessible.

The western lead district embraces Hickory, Dallas, Polk, St. Clair, Cedar and Dade counties. Some rich deposits have been found in this district, especially in Hickory county.

The southwestern lead district comprises Jasper, Newton, Lawrence, Stone, Barry and McDonald. Here very extensive mining has been done, more especially in the two counties first named, which have, for the last few years, produced more than one-half of the pig lead mined in the State. The famous mines in the Granby and Joplin districts have, in a few years, made those counties increase immensely in population. Many lead furnaces are in active operation, and the industry is an important source of wealth. These mines are surrounded by a rich agricultural region, and the one industry has materially assisted in the development of the other.

For several years past more than one-half the lead production of the United States has been from Missouri mines. Besides the numerous smelting works supported by them, the manufacture of white lead, lead pipe, sheet lead, etc., contributes materially to the industries and commerce of the State.

The amount of mining in southwestern Missouri amazes one who has not been familiar with the developments. For miles a line of stacks meets his view, and he is surrounded by the most valuable mines in the country. On the site where lead ore was first discovered, 15 years ago, a 40-acre tract brings to its owner a royalty of $50,000 a year. For a single acre lot, $60,000 has been refused, and the parties, by holding, have cleared $300,000, and are still working at a profit. The only thing necessary for persons to accrue an immense fortune in this district is to buy large tracts and hold them for development. This region has been well named the poor man's country and the rich man's paradise. Many poor men have reached the mines without money to buy a pick or shovel, windlass or bucket, who have afterwards become very wealthy. The smelters buy the ore at the mines and haul it away. Each week the royalty to the land owner is deposited to his credit in bank, thus requiring no personal supervision or presence.

ZINC.

It is not very widely known that Missouri produces nearly three-fourths of the zinc consumed in the United States annually, and still less is known even within the borders of the State itself of the mines which produce this great output. Passing over and through the Ozark mountain range, to the southwest of St. Louis, and far out on their western slope, and on the Lexington & Southern division of the Missouri Pacific railway, will be found the flourishing little cities of Carthage, Joplin and Webb City. These are the commercial centers of the zinc and lead mining districts of southwest Missouri, and it is in their immediate vicinity that the greater part of the former metal is mined. The two counties of Newton and Jasper embrace the greater part of the region from which this very valuable mineral is dug.

The zinc mines of Missouri are only a recent discovery. Fifteen years ago the present site of the principal mines of Webb City was offered for $15 per acre, but the wife refused to sign the deed. Now the royalty on forty acres of this tract amounts to $50,000 per year at the rate of seven and one-half per cent. On this same mineral belt there are single acre lots of 200 feet square that have produced in royalties, with no expense to the owners of the land, over $100,000. A single mine nine years ago sold for $325. Three years ago it sold for $14,000, and the present owners have just refused $900 per acre for the 40 acres.

A strange feature of the mineral is that lead ore is found above the zinc ore, and wherever lead ore is found, zinc ore is found beneath it, leading to the conclusion that lead ore is the result of some chemical action produced by the zinc ore.

At Galena, about ten miles from Webb City, the entire tract was traded for a pony not many years ago. Eight acres of this have paid the owners a royalty of over $200,000, and an eighty acre tract adjoining has made the owners immensely wealthy, having paid them over half a million royalty. This is not the corporation and capitalist's mining country exclusively. The region has been well named the "Poor man's country and the Rich man's Paradise." Without exception every dooryard is a dump pile, a shaft in the center, with rope and windlass. Shafts are worked at a profit on lots 25x100 feet. Two hundred feet square is considered a miner's lot. Without expense to the owner of the land, miners will sink a shaft and operate, paying the owner one-fifth royalty.

A person not visiting the country can have no conception of the opportunities for profitable investment. There is an entire absence of speculation. People in the East, who have been content with investments paying six, seven and eight per cent, can scarcely credit the statements relative to the wonderful opportunities for sure, safe and very profitable investments in the lead and zinc district of Missouri.

The mining interests are just in their infancy, although the product already exceeds $2,000,000 annually. The people are just awakening to the value of their property. At the same time mineral land can still be secured at reasonable prices from those who cannot appreciate at this time their prospective value, and who are satisfied with what they consider a large profit on land—which to-day sells at from $35 to $100 per acre—

A COUNTRY FORD. OZARK MOUNTAINS.

which entry secured a few years ago at comparatively insignificant prices from the government. Much of the land when located was purchased from the government at a shilling an acre, and $50 represents an enormous advance, while the same land as soon as developed often changes hands at $10,000 to $50,000 an acre. The sulphurate of zinc, known among miners as black jack, is often found in such quantities as to retard the progress of lead mining, and from the expense of getting the ores to the smelting works, it has been thrown out in dumps, and much of it left as worthless matter. This was formerly the case. But by the completion of railroads, giving better transportation facilities, this ore has become valuable merchandise. The increase of railroad facilities, and the fact that sixteen new smelters will be erected this year, speaks volumes for the permanency of the mining interests of this region and their greater development in the near future.

COPPER, GRANITE AND OTHER MINERALS.

The mountains and hills of Missouri are filled with nearly every variety of minerals, and among them are found numerous outcroppings of copper, mainly in Dent, Crawford, Benton, Maries, Greene, Lawrence, Dade, Taney, Dallas, Phelps, Reynolds, Wright and Washington counties. Some of these outcroppings have been worked with varying success from time to time, but owing to lack of capital, well directed effort and facilities for shipping, the copper industry of Missouri is very little developed. There is no doubt that copper exists in paying quantities in many localities in the State and will in the near future bring good returns to investors. At present the only mines of copper that are successfully worked are located in southeast Missouri, in Washington and St. Genevieve counties. Some of the mines in Shannon county are now profitably worked and mines in Franklin county have yielded good results.

The sandstones, granites, limestones and marbles of the State supply an abundance of fine and durable stone for all building and architectural uses. Sandstones are found in many beautiful shades of brown, red and buff, which are easily worked when taken from the quarries and harden upon exposure. The granites of Missouri are equal to any in the world for building and paving purposes. They are solid and beautiful. The red granite makes as beautiful and ornamental building and monumental stones as the celebrated Scotch granite. The finest and most substantial structures of St. Louis and Kansas City are built of granite and sandstones taken from the mines of the State.

)*Fire Clays* underlie a large portion of the State and the manufacture of fire-bricks, gas retorts and other articles requiring the most refractory clays, has long been successfully carried on in St. Louis county. These clays occur here in the lower coal series and exist in great quantities. There are many beds of these clays found in the counties north of the

Missouri river, and their quality is almost beyond computation. The most of them possess very fine refractory properties. Fire rock has also been found in abundance, some of the silicious beds of the coal measures being very refractory.

In addition to the foregoing large quantities of glass is manufactured from the deposits of kaolin in the eastern part of the State, and potters' clays, limestones, marble, tin, nickel, manganese, cobalt and paints are found in paying quantities.

Missouri's greatest wealth lies beneath her soil and locked up in her hills and mountains. In manufacturing, Missouri should rival Pennsylvania, and should be a wealthier and greater State because of its greater agricultural resources.

AS TO FRUIT.

AS a fruit State Missouri stands without a parallel. California is justly celebrated in this respect, but the value of the fruit crop of Missouri annually exceeds that of California. It is not given to the production of one kind of fruit, but all varieties flourish equally well. The apple is as much at home here as in New York State, and the peach is not surpassed even by Delaware's celebrated product. Her vineyards and their products in quantity and quality can compete with the world.

The latitude of Missouri, between the 36th and 40th parallels is better adapted for successful fruit growing than is the country either north or south of it. Here peaches flourish as they do in few of the Northern States, while many tender fruits, such as apricots, nectarines, figs and many of the choicer varieties of grapes can be grown with ordinary care, and the fruits of the North, apples, pears, plums and cherries, grow here equally well with very much less trouble and care, all the labor of protecting the trees from the biting frost of a long cold winter being quite unnecessary, as the winters are so much shorter and less severe than the New England season of frost and snow.

Fruit culture in Missouri is still in its infancy; yet great progress has been already made. None of the catalogue of fruits adapted to this latitude fail of success in this State. Every owner of a lot of ground in almost every portion of the State can, with a small outlay of money and labor, raise all the fruit required for family consumption, from the strawberry and early cherry to the late keeping apple, and thousands of acres could, with a reasonable amount of labor properly bestowed, be converted into fine fruit gardens and orchards. The adaptation and capacity of Missouri to produce fruit for market and for transportation are unsurpassed. There is no question of the profit of raising apples for market, if a proper location is selected, good varieties planted, and reasonable care bestowed on the trees and on the fruit after it is gathered.

Where other fruits grow so finely, apples, of all fruits the most interesting to settlers, cannot fail to succeed. The apples of Missouri are of remarkably fine color and size and many varieties flourish here so much better than in the East, that Eastern fruit growers often fail to recognize varieties with which they have had life long acquaintance, when Missouri calls their attention to improved and enlarged editions of the old time sorts. To locate the most favorable district for apple culture would be impossible. Those who have visited nearly every part of the State and made extensive observations among our fruit growers say they have yet to learn of a single orchard, with even the let-alone cultivation so common in the West, which has not been a source of profit to the owner.

Pears do well throughout the State, especially in the region of Clay, Jackson and Cass counties. The tree attains a great size and age—a diameter of from twelve to fifteen inches is common—and the fruit is borne in great profusion and is very luscious.

The Southeastern portion of the State, along the line of the St. Louis, Iron Mountain & Southern railway, and in the western and southern portion where the marly deposits are so rich and extensive, are pre-eminently the peach districts, and in these regions the peach seems almost indigenous, never failing to produce most abundant crops; and yet fruit growers of these districts say they are unable to supply the demand from Nebraska, Kansas, Colorado, and from the great fruit market of St. Louis. Peaches may be relied upon as a profitable and sure crop in all that part of the State south of the Missouri river, and they are also successfully grown in the northern division of the State.

But it is as a grape growing State that Missouri ranks above all others. Other States may compete with her in other fruits, but in grape culture she is the acknowledged leader, and Missouri grape growers have done

MISSOURI.

more to advance this branch of horticulture in the United States than those of all other States combined. Missouri is the native habitat of the grape. Wild vines grow to great dimensions, sometimes reaching ten and twelve inches in diameter. Some of these have been cultivated with

ON THE MERAMEC, MOUTH OF KEIFFER CREEK. MISSOURI PACIFIC RAILWAY

great success with the result of adding several valuable varieties to the list of standard grapes. These have an excellent adaptation to wine making. Missouri has originated more new varieties than any other

State and that her wines are of superior quality is attested by the fact that since its advent as a wine-making State, Missouri wines have received the highest awards at every world's fair.

The native varieties of grapes while producing the best quality of clarets, Burgundies and sherries, are free from the grape blight, known as phylloxera, which has been so disastrous to the wine interests of France and lately has invaded California. There is consequently a great demand for cullings from Missouri vines, which has been a source of revenue to the vinters of the State. The material is in Missouri to-day to compete with France and Burgundy in their choicest red wines and with the Rhine and Moselle in their best hocks.

While therefore the prospects of Missouri grape growers rest upon a surer basis than ever before, while the American grape grower feels assured of a grand success, the prospects of France, Germany, and in short all the grape-growing districts of Europe, are darkening. The shortage in the annual vintage increases with each year while the demand is steadily on the increase. The demand must be met. The wine growers of Europe must leave their devastated and uncertain vineyards. Let them bring their skill and industry here and supply the demand that the failing vineyards are sure to create. There are millions and millions of acres of land in this State that can produce the wines. Men who are willing to work and wait a few years for the results of their labor are wanted; men who have sense, skill and industry enough to profit by the experience of those who have worked before them, who can adapt themselves to the different requirements of this climate.

While possessing the natural advantages of soil and climate, there is still another advantage in fruit growing which Missouri possesses and that is a market near to home for all she can raise. It is located farthest to the westward of all the fruit States east of the Rocky Mountains. The States west with their hot dry climate, in which it is impossible to grow perfect fruit, stand ready to absorb the supply before it can reach the mining regions of the Rocky Mountains, where the demand for fruit is so great that it would consume the whole production were the State planted in one vast orchard and still ask for more.

There are few parts of this great State from which fruit cannot find direct and convenient transportation to a market which is never overstocked. All roads lead to St. Louis which is the greatest fruit market of the West. Then in later years there have sprung up on the west, the great consuming centers of Kansas City and St. Joseph, which annually require a great and ever increasing supply. Besides these mammoth market places, the fruit growers of Missouri can ship their surplus to Iowa, Minnesota and Dakota where there is growing up an enormous demand for it. A great population is growing up in the western fruitless region which must be supplied and Missouri will always have the advantage of location in meeting the demand from this source. From the western portion of the State there are direct lines of transportation to the mines in the West, and the southern and southeastern sections have their capacity taxed to the utmost, to supply the needs of Texas and the rapidly growing Southwest which part of the country is reached by the Iron Mountain route.

All these can be safely sent hundreds of miles to market and the great network of railroads radiating from St. Louis, and permeating the country in every direction, enables the fruit growers of Missouri to sell their products to the inhabitants of all that vast money-making, non-fruit-growing, but fruit-consuming country extending westward to the Rocky Mountains, and from British America to Mexico, and to find a profitable market in the States north, northwest and northeast of them.

Perhaps no better proof can be given of the grand excellence of Missouri fruits than the fact that at several late meetings of the American Pomological Society, medals were awarded to Missouri for the best display of apples, pears and wines, and also for the best general display of fruits, gaining these honors when in competition with every State in the Union, represented by their choicest fruits. One of these meetings was held at Rochester, N. Y., which has long been regarded as the very center of the fruit growing interests of the country. At the St. Louis Exposition in the fall of 1888, the Southwest Missouri Immigration Society had an exhibit of apples that surpassed anything ever gotten together for a local display.

CONCERNING LANDS.

MISSOURI may be classed among the older States, having been made one of the Union in 1821. It may, therefore, be taken for granted that there is not a large quantity of public lands, either State or government, still remaining open for homesteads. The railroads were induced to construct lines through the State in its earlier years, by the donation of large tracts of land. These, also, as in the case of government lands, are nearly exhausted. There is some still remaining, and a small portion of government land in southeast Missouri, which will be taken up and treated under headings of their own.

The great inducements for coming to Missouri lie, not in the free government lands and cheap railroad lands, but in the low price of well improved and excellent farming lands, near to through lines of railroad and in close proximity to first-class markets. Missouri, during the whole period of its existence as a State, has done very little to induce immigration by setting off the advantages of the State agriculturally, or in letting the world know what it had to offer in the way of making money and homes, to those who had money to invest and industry and enterprise to acquire a competence. The State has grown slowly, because the process of finding out its worth has been slow. People, by gradually finding out in a slow way, by handing from one to another, what Missouri is, have come in, acquired wealth, and pushed the State, with their unaided efforts and scarcely without the knowledge of the outside world, into the third rank in agricultural resources and wealth. Very few realize, outside of the State, that Missouri stands third in the value of agricultural products. Yet such is the case, and it is all the more astonishing when it is taken into consideration how much of her resources are still undeveloped, and many, as yet, untouched. It is a matter of wonder, too, that so prominent and successful an agricultural State should reach its proud position and her general farming lands, from which her wealth is derived, remain so cheap. It is a fact well known that much of the improved land of Missouri can be obtained at figures at least as low, if not lower, than land several hundred miles farther west, on the extreme frontiers of civilization, where there are none of the advantages of schools, churches, railroads, cities and towns, and well organized and excellent society. The Missouri lands are cheap, and have improvements which will only come to the frontiersman by years of labor under the greatest drawbacks. There, there is no building material or timber. Missouri is overflowing with it. Fuel must be brought from a long distance, and can be had only at high prices. In Missouri the cost of fuel is almost nothing. In Missouri there is fruit in plenty and all the luxuries of a comfortable home life on the farm.

We have said that it was in the cheapness of general farming lands of

PILOT KNOB VILLAGE AND MOUNTAIN, IRON MOUNTAIN ROUTE.

the State that the inducements to immigration mostly lie. The general price of land, except near to the larger cities, is low. No State, so well surrounded by good markets and so near the great centers of commerce, and with such complete systems of traffic thoroughfares, and with such great manufacturing centers within its borders, shows such a discrepancy between its land values and great natural and commercial advantages.

Of course there is a great range in land values here as elsewhere. Much of the land is broken and rocky, and fit only for pasturage, and there can be no better for this purpose. The famous dairy regions of New York are not better adapted by nature for dairying than are the hill and valley lands of central southern Missouri. This can be made the dairy region of the West. The price of these lands at present is a mere bagatelle, and the best of pasture lands, with abundance of water and shelter, can be purchased for from $3.00 to $7.00 per acre.

The lands adapted to general crop raising range considerably higher than the preceding, but are still fabulously low, considering their quality and productiveness. If you are about to move West you are warned to beware of excursions into the wilderness. You will pass through some of the most fertile agricultural regions in the country, where failure of crops is almost unknown, where markets are convenient and agriculture profitable. You will pay nearly as much per acre for semi-improved land on the frontiers of civilization as for land in Missouri which is all under cultivation and provided with house and stables that would require nearly as great an outlay as the original cost of the farm, owing to the scarcity of timber and high price of building materials. Good farming lands in Missouri may be purchased as low as $18 per acre that will produce all the grains and fruits of the United States. And the prices range from this amount up to $50 per acre for land in the choicest localities. The very best of farming land near to markets and railroads can be purchased for $20, $25 and $30 per acre, on which can be raised as much grain, hay and other produce as on the $100 acre farms of Ohio, New York and Pennsylvania.

EXEMPTION AND TAXATION LAWS.

It will be of interest to the home-seeker who contemplates taking up his abode in Missouri to be acquainted with the safeguards which the laws of the State throw around the workingman to protect him from the encroachments of money lenders.

The laws of Missouri reserve from execution, in the hands of every head of a family living in the country, a homestead, consisting of one hundred and sixty (160) acres of land, not exceeding $1,500 in value; to every head of a family, in cities of over 40,000 inhabitants, a homestead, consisting of not more than thirty square rods of ground, and of the value of not more than $1,500. Thus, it is seen, that a farmer's homestead in Missouri consists of one hundred and sixty acres of land and the improvements thereon, not exceeding in value $1,500; the homesteads of the residents of the smaller towns are of the same value; while that allowed to the inhabitants of St. Louis, St. Joseph and Kansas City, where land is more valuable and the cost of living greater, is fixed at $3,000.

The Constitution places it beyond the power of reckless or dishonest public agents to burden the people with excessive taxation. Taxes for State purposes, exclusive of the taxes necessary to pay the bonded debt

A REMINISCENCE.

of the State, cannot exceed twenty cents on the hundred dollars valuation; and whenever the taxable property of the State shall amount to $900,000,000, the rate shall not exceed fifteen cents. The rate of taxation for county, city, town and school purposes is likewise strictly limited. Counties, cities, towns, townships and school districts cannot become indebted beyond the revenue provided for each year, without a two-thirds vote of all voters therein, nor, in any event, to an amount exceeding five per cent on the value of taxable property.

THE TIMBER OF MISSOURI.

MISSOURI is not so densely and thoroughly timbered as some other States, and yet its resources in this respect are by no means inconsiderable. In truth, Missouri makes a very creditable showing in the amount and variety of her standing timber, as behooves a great State singularly blessed in respect of natural advantages. Possibly one-fourth of the total area north of the Missouri river is forest land, and one-half of that south of the same stream. The general line of demarkation between the prairie and timbered sections cannot be described to a nicety, because even the extreme western parts of the State are dotted, and its streams fringed, with forests of greater or less magnitude; but, for all practical purposes, that part of the State lying east of a line drawn from Hannibal to Jefferson City, and thence south to the Arkansas border in Stone county, may be regarded as the more heavily timbered section. Over this large area are to be found an almost infinite variety of hardwoods, besides yellow pine in the direction of Arkansas, and many of the woods that are technically "soft." For instance, there are three sorts of locust, three of walnut, four of maple, four of gum, six of hickory and eighteen of oak.

The distribution of the different species of wood is admirable, on the whole, for mill work. There are regions of many miles in area over which only one or two, and certainly not more than three or four, varieties occur. In the counties of Mississippi, Stoddard, Scott, Pemiscot, Dunklin, New Madrid and Butler, in southeastern Missouri, the prevailing timber is white oak, gum, poplar, cypress and one or two varieties of ash. The oak of this region is among the best found in the State, and the gums are beginning to be used to a large extent now as a substitute for black walnut for many uses. The pine timber lands extend through Jefferson and Washington counties in a southeasterly, southerly and southwesterly direction, embracing Madison, Wayne and the northern part of Butler on the east, touching the Arkansas line in Ripley county. To the westward they pass through Reynolds, Carter, Shannon, Oregon,

Howard, Texas, Douglas, Ozark and Taney counties. The hillsides and valleys in some of these counties are also well timbered with oak, hickory and ash.

Much of the timber of Missouri is exceptionally valuable, as a recent writer on the subject points out. The swamp oak, for example, which is abundant in the southern part of the State, is the best variety of wood used for ship-building, with the single exception of live oak. Cypress, which also occurs in the extreme southern counties, is, of course, known to be a "coming wood." The growth of the forests in this State are, moreover, very heavy in some districts. Pine on the plateaus of Shannon, Carter, Reynolds, Oregon and Howell counties averages, in many places, from 8,000 to 10,000 feet to the acre. Ash, oak, maple and walnut are also dense, and heavy over large regions. Sycamores have been found in the State measuring 43 feet in circumference and 65 feet in height, if we may trust the statement, and cottonwoods have grown to a height of 125 feet, with a girth of 30 feet. Some very large Spanish oak, black walnut and cypress trees have also been cut in the lower portion of the State.

On the southern slope of the Ozark range, west of the belt of oak forests in eastern Missouri, along the line of the Iron Mountain Railway, is a rich belt of yellow pine covering the two southeasternmost tiers of counties of the State. Fully 65 per cent of the area is yellow pine. It is of the short leaf variety, is remarkably free from resin and turpentine, and the lumber made from it well adapted for the interior finishing of houses. There are many magnificent trees in this region, and 4,000 to 6,000 feet of lumber are now cut to the acre, leaving the smaller growth intact.

The timber in southern Missouri varies with the latitude. In the southeastern portion of the State the poplar, the sweet, black and yellow gum, the pine and cypress, the birch, the beech and the tulip tree have their home, and one scarcely, if ever, found in the northern or western counties, but through the entire region of southern Missouri. The forest trees are oak, walnut and hickory, elm, maple, ash and locust, with their varieties, cherry, cottonwood, willow, persimmon, pecan, hackberry, mulberry, box elder, sassafras, growing to tree size, and, in the southwest, the chestnut and the chinquepin.

A bill has been introduced in the State Legislature at Jefferson City providing for the incorporating of booming companies on the rivers of Missouri, especially on the Current river, the principal and lowest town on which is Doniphan.

SCENE IN THE TIMBER REGION, SOUTHEAST MISSOURI.

This plan is feasible and practical, and, if no opposition be made to it, it will, doubtless, be carried out sooner or later. The estimate, 400,000 car-loads, of the lumber in easy reach of Current river is probably no exaggeration. The forests in this section are immense and the timber is of the finest and of the best varieties. As the matter now stands, the greater part is naturally tributary to St. Louis, and, with the proper efforts on the part of St. Louis capitalists, the trade would preponderate in favor of that place.

Doniphan is the largest town on Current river. It is situated ten miles north of the Arkansas line and immediately below the great pine belt. It is 200 miles from St. Louis, and is in direct railroad communication with it by means of the Doniphan Branch of the St. Louis, Iron Mountain & Southern Railway. It has a great advantage over any other point on Current river in the fact that it is below all the pine and most of the hard timber tributary to that river. Every log in reach of the river for 100 miles up could be rafted to this place, sawed and shipped directly to St. Louis. Every log that can be boomed at Van Buren or Eminence could also be floated to this place, while for a distance of 35 miles above here no railroad touches the river, and the vast amount of timber in that belt can be shipped only through this place. Some of the larger creeks which run back into the pineries afford facilities for running logs into the river for considerable distances back in the hills during high water, notably Big Barren creek, which empties into the river twenty miles above here.

The valley of this creek extends 20 or 25 miles up into the heart of one of the finest pineries in the Union, which as yet is untouched. By cleaning out and straightening the channel of this creek, it could be made, during heavy rains, the means of getting all this timber to the river, and thence to the railroad at Doniphan.

But the timber does not consist solely of pine. Vast quantities of hard timber, especially oak, is in reach of this place. To show the resources of this section in this particular, it is only necessary to cite what has been done in the hard timber land on the Doniphan Branch, 20 miles long. Since its building six years ago millions of ties and staves, and piling and lumber, in immense quantities, have been shipped over it, and still all the good oak timber within handling distance of the road is not nearly exhausted.

Ash, hickory and gum are also in reach of this place. No better point could be selected for the establishment of wood factories, mills, etc. It is true that there is to be an enormous business done in this section of Missouri at no distant date, and some city or cities will derive great benefit from it. Capital is all that is needed to develop it.

ADAPTABILITY TO MANUFACTURES

HISTORY teaches that a people who with raw products alone attempt to contest for wealth and population against a people elaborating these products are sure to be worsted.

Missouri is important in having a swift creator of wealth, the most important demand of all active civilizations, an unlimited water power, in addition to the raw materials for manufacturing all the essentials of American civilization, wool, cotton, timber, iron, copper, lead, zinc, coal, the raw material for paper, and many other minerals shown under a separate heading. In this element of wealth, cheap motive power, this State is rich indeed. Not in all the Eastern States can there be found such a rolling, rapid river as the Gasconade, about 85 miles from St. Louis. Here every two miles or less there is sufficient fall to raise a dam that would afford power enough to run 500 looms. Magnificent powers are lying idle on the Osage, Grand river, Meramec, Black, White, St. Francis, Current, and numberless other streams within the borders of the State, and there is, perhaps, one of the grandest possible water powers in the West or South almost under the shadow of St. Louis.

It is believed to be practicable to tap the Missouri river at or near Tavern Rock, in western part of St. Louis county, and to construct an artificial waterway down the valley by the way of and taking in its course Creve Cœur lake, only 26 miles from the city, where a fall of fully 32 feet could be secured to the banks of the Des Peres, or even pass through the southern portion of the city of St. Louis and empty into the Mississippi river above the mouth of the Des Peres. This would afford power equal to any now utilized in New England, and enable the factories on its banks the entire distance to stand within one mile or less of each other, without interference from back water. Here twenty cotton and woolen mills could be erected, backed by superior location and facilities offered by the city of St. Louis.

Creve Cœur lake is a large body of beautiful soft water, free of the metaloids that unfit it for bleaching goods and manufacture of paper. These industries would find here an admirable location, especially the paper mills. Materials for its manufacture are produced all around the lake, and poplar, that now furnishes about seventy-five per cent of the material for manufacture of books and newspapers, grows in great abundance within a very few miles of the spot where the mills would be erected. The balance of paper material, straw, rags and cotton waste would be supplied from the farms and mills and the markets of St. Louis, all very close at hand. Platin creek, 20 miles below St. Louis, is a beautiful stream of pure water, flowing from a sandstone bluff, soft as rain water; is an admirable location for bleaching goods and the manufacture of paper; is accessible by the Mississippi river, into which it flows, and the Iron Mountain Route, which crosses it about 10 miles above its mouth, by which material and manufactured goods could reach the mills, and goods shipped to St. Louis at a small cost. Besides these rare advantages of water powers, no State perhaps, in the American Union has such extensive coal beds to be found in almost every county in the State—aggregating 22,000 square miles of coal of excellent quality—mined so easily and cheaply as to make the use of steam in propelling machinery almost as cheap as water power. Cheap fuel for steam and general family uses would enable manufacturers to erect works in a majority of the cities and towns of Missouri where operatives have their homes, and children working in the factories could live with their parents and add to the family revenue by the labor they perform in the cotton and woolen mills.

Here manufacturers have the great advantage of a home market for articles turned out of looms and furnaces. St. Louis has been for years a full port for entry and appraisement. The ability of her merchants to duplicate any bill of foreign goods purchased on the Atlantic seaboard has drawn to her a class of buyers that hitherto purchased only in the markets of the East. This has greatly augmented her trade in domestic fabrics, and to-day she is the largest market in the Mississippi Valley for such goods.

They would be located where the material to manufacture is produced, or is collected without cost of transportation. In close proximity food for operatives is produced and delivered without commission, transportation, interest or exchange, and, not the least important, they would have a home market for nearly all of the goods they can produce. Not having

FALLS OF EVANGELINE,
NEAR ARCADIA.
IRON MOUNTAIN ROUTE

three frieghts to pay on material, food and on manufactured products, they could undersell the mills of the East, that are compelled to pay these inevitable charges.

In view of these facts and advantages, Missouri invites capital and machinery to settle within her environs. Her manufacturers are assured of a ready sale for all the goods a dozen mills could produce, and at such prices and saving in production as will pay a magnificent dividend on capital wisely expended. The wholesale jobbers are, without exception, anxious to see such mills established in Missouri, and will, at all times, give preference to home-made products over goods made outside of the State.

It is apparent that the manufacturing industries are capable of great legitimate expansion. The importation of articles that might be manufactured at a profit in the State, and thus supply the home market, is very large. The people are alive to fostering this branch of commercial interest, and, at all times, extend a welcome and, in many instances, substantial assistance to the manufacturing capitalist.

SOMETHING FOR THE SPORTSMAN.

MISSOURI has been the feeding ground for vast herds of the choicest of the large game animals up to the present generation. Old hunters and trappers still living tell marvelous, but true, stories of their exploits with the gun. As civilization and population advanced westward their numbers decreased, yet Missouri is still furnishing a very large proportion of the game for the markets of all the large cities of the United States. From October 1st to February 1st of every year there is not an express car arriving in St. Louis which does not bring large consignments of game. The quantity is enormous and far beyond the knowledge of every one except those engaged in the trade, or whose duties bring them in contact with the fact. Deer are found in every portion of the State, and are especially numerous in the thinly settled, hilly and mountainous districts. They are also numerous in the swampy districts. The Ozark mountains and the swampy lands of southeast Missouri constitute a great deer park and game reserve and will continue to do so until immigration crowds them out. It is a notorious fact that venison sells as cheap as good beef in the St. Louis markets during the winter season.

Game in the Ozarks of all kinds is most plentiful. It is a striking indication to the sportsman to see the skins of deer, wild cats, foxes, 'coons, 'possums and minks hanging on the posts of the porticos in front of the country stores, while the skins of bears and wolves are not infrequent. These skins tell an unmistakable story of the sport which the hunter can find in Missouri. The truth is that small game is so plentiful that it is practically ignored by the natives.

IDEAL HUNTING GROUNDS, MISSOURI

In response to an inquiry a native said:

"Did anyone thereabouts go gunning for game? Right smart of folks did that. What did they kill? Most generally deer. The railroad brought right smart of folks from St. Louis gunning through that country. What else did they get besides deer? Turkeys. City folks sot a heap of store by turkeys, out folks didn't bother 'em very much less there was a workin's and meat was skeerse and no time to kill a deer. There was droves of turkeys up the river. How far? 'Bout two mile. It was scandalous the way them 'ud rassle with a farmer's corn. He'd as lief have a drove of hogs in a corn field as a flock of turkeys, and there wa'nt no keeping of them out. Partridges? Never see none. Quail? Do you 'uns shoot quail? Well I reckon they's tolable good eatin', but taint a mouthful apiece skeersely to the little things."

The truth is that wild turkeys are nowhere more plentiful in the United States than in the Ozark mountains. What, with the acorns and other "mast," mild winters, the great stretches of unsettled lands, and the indifference of the native sportsman, turkeys thrive like barnyard fowls in Jersey. Nor is it necessary to lie in wait in a blind and call them to get a shot. It is as easy to get a shot at a turkey as to get a shot at a partridge in the Pennsylvania woods.

SHEEP PASTURE.
SOUTHWEST MISSOURI.
MISSOURI PACIFIC RAILWAY.

As for squirrels and rabbits, they everywhere abound. There is but one drawback to the shooting of small game in this country It is so tame as to take the zest out of the sport. Except for the pleasure of having a well-stocked larder, there is no fun in shooting small game. However, if a man were to come here armed with a 20-bore double shot-gun and cartridges loaded with two drachms of powder

MISSOURI.

and three-fourths of an ounce of say No. 8 shot, he could kill all the game he could carry without mutilating it. But if one would have real sport with small game a 22-calibre rifle would be the thing, and enough straightaway shots could be had at quail to enable a fairly good shot to fill a game bag.

The deer are usually run into the river with dogs, as they are in the Adirondacks. This plan is adopted because it is less laborious than still hunting. The dogs do the traveling, while the sportsman sits down on the river bank and rests.

One might travel over a very wild region without finding a more lovely place to rest in than a nook on the banks of White river. The hills and mountains, when dressed in the varying shades of brown and gray, are scarcely less beautiful than in the fresh bloom of spring. The sky has the blue haze of Indian summer and the air is as invigorating as a sea breeze in August. The water of the river is so pure and clear that one may count the stones  on the bottom ten feet below the surface. There is even a charm in the naked white limbs of the sycamore that reach out in all directions like ghostly arms striving to clasp something as the wind sways them.

Deer are very easily stalked here in the right weather. The weather is right immediately after or during a rain storm or a snow storm. Snow often falls to a depth of six inches, and sometimes remains several days. When the leaves are well soaked with water one may dress in a suit of brown, and, with rubber shoes instead of boots, walk within range of the deer without difficulty. Of course they are not as tame as the turkeys and quail. In the vernacular here, "they are not so —— tame, jest tame." They are commonly hunted with shot-guns, the rifle being reserved for squirrels, and, in case it is a repeater, for men.

The country abounds in foxes and wild cats, however, the foxes being the more numerous, of course. Both sorts of brutes grow fat on fur and feather. Naturally, the 'coon and the 'possum are still more numerous.

The way for Eastern people to go shooting in this country is to go as far as they can by rail and then hire what they call a freighter's wagon and a driver who can cook. Into the wagon pack sufficient supplies to last as long as the hunters desire to stay. The supply need not include feed for the horses, for corn and "roughness," which is the localism for fodder, are to be cheaply and conveniently obtained from the natives. The camp is not likely to be made further than five miles from a supply of corn and fodder. From $2 to $2.75 a day will pay for the driver and his rig, if one does not go to a livery stable. Plain food is much cheaper here than in the East. The transient rate for travelers at hotels is $1 a day. By the month the price is from $10 to $12, and that for good food and clean lodgings; so the expenses of camping out would be very low indeed if high-priced canned goods were not brought from the city.

Prairie chickens are found exclusively in the prairie regions of Missouri, which embrace nearly one-half of the State. They are shipped from Missouri to Eastern and other markets in vast numbers. Quail, the gamest of birds, abounds in all parts of Missouri. Their favorite haunts being in and around farms, the numbers are increasing as the number of farms multiply. This bird is a general favorite with farmers, sportsmen and epicures and gives more pleasure than any other game.

The early settlers found the rivers and lakes teeming with many fine varieties of food and game fish. There is still a bountiful supply, but of course not as great as when the State was more thinly settled.

Black bass, perch, croppie, cat fish, buffalo fish, suckers and pike constitute the leading varieties of native fish.

Black bass of several varieties inhabit every stream of considerable size in the State.

The perch family is represented by several dozen species, and perch of several kinds are found in every body of water in the State which does not actually dry up in the summer.

MISSOURI. 37

The cat fish of Missouri are not only numerous, but famous the world over. There are at least a dozen species in the waters of this State. They vary in size from 1 to 100 pounds. The cat fish is a good food fish, but so common that it is not appreciated.

The buffalo fish is the largest of the numerous sucker family in this State. They often attain a weight of twenty pounds and upwards. It is a good food fish and is found in every portion of the State.

Pike of several species are found throughout Missouri and rank with black bass as game fish. They are found in the clearer and rapid streams.

The above list constitutes the leading fish of the State, but by no means all, as there are many minor species.

EDUCATION AND SCHOOLS.

IT has been asserted by some and assumed by others, who do not know the facts, that a public spirit of opposition to free schools dominates legislation in Missouri. On the other hand, Missourians claim that no policy of government is more firmly rooted in the affections of the people or more securely established than the purpose to extend the advantages of a liberal education to all classes.

No State in the American Union has ever manifested more zeal in the cause of popular education than Missouri, nor is her present attitude the manifestation of a new impulse. When she began her existence as a State she began an earnest effort in behalf of education, and there has been no abatement of that effort, unless the unavoidable interruption of the course of events during the civil war be so regarded; and he who charges that the State is opposed to free schools, or ever has been, is challenged to name that State which fills his ideal, educationally, and invited to a comparison of the temper of the two States on the subject.

The third proposition of the Act of Congress of March 6th, 1820, permitting Missouri Territory to form a State government, declared that five per cent of the net proceeds of the sales of public lands within the territory should be reserved, after January, 1821, for making roads and canals, three-fifths to be used in the State, and two-fifths in constructing a road or roads to the State.

The convention which assembled in July, 1820, in pursuance of this act of Congress, requested such a modification of this proposition as would permit the whole of the five per cent to be used in the State for the purposes named "and the promotion of education in the State." Thus the people of Missouri manifested a solicitude for the education of their children in the outset of the State government. And when it is remembered that Congress had offered and they had accepted the magnificent gifts of the sixteenth section of every township of land for schools of those townships, and thirty-six sections of land for the use of a seminary of learning (the State University), the request for further aid in this direction shows that they regarded the question of education as one of transcendent importance.

The article on education in the Constitution of 1820 (Art. VI.) contained only two sections. The first section provided that "schools and the means of education shall forever be encouraged in this State," and directed the Legislature to preserve the school lands from waste and to apply the proceeds of any sales which should be made "in strict conformity to the object of the grant." It also directed that one or more schools should be established in every township as soon as practicable (that is, as soon as there were sufficient funds on hand) and necessary. The second section provided for the care of the seminary or university lands.

The article on education in the Constitution, adopted in 1865 (Art. IX.), has nine sections. The first reads "A general diffusion of knowledge and intelligence being essential to the preservation of the rights and liberties of the people, the General Assembly shall establish and maintain free schools for the gratuitous instruction of all persons in this State between the ages of 5 and 21 years."

Section 2 provides that separate schools for children of African descent may be established.

Section 3 creates a Board of Education, to consist of the State Superintendent, Secretary of State and Attorney-General.

Section 4 provides for maintenance of the University, with departments in teaching, in agriculture and in natural science.

Section 5 describes and perpetuates the public school fund and directs the application of its income.

Section 6 requires the State fund to be invested only in United States bonds (amended in 1870 so as to permit investment in Missouri State bonds) and the county funds to be loaned.

Section 7 requires the maintenance of schools for at least three months in the year as the condition of receiving any part of the income of the public school fund, and permits the Legislature to provide for compulsory education.

Section 8 provides for local taxation for schools.

Section 9 provides for the reduction of lands, money or other property held for school purposes into the public school fund.

The article on education in the Constitution adopted in 1875 (Art. XI.) contains eleven sections. The first is an exact reproduction of the same section of the Constitution of 1865, except a change of school age from between 5 and 21 to between 6 and 20.

Section 4 adds the Governor to the State Board of Education.

Section 7 requires the annual appropriation of 25 per cent of the State's revenues, exclusive of the interest and sinking funds, for the maintenance of schools. (This is the first appearance in the organic law of a provision for the ordinary revenue to education.)

Section 11 forbids the appropriation of any public money in aid of any religious creed, church or sectarian purpose, or to sustain any school controlled by any religious creed, church or sectarian denomination.

These, with a few minor and immaterial changes, and with better provisions for the State University, are the only additions to the same article of the Constitution of 1865.

But Section 43 of Article IV., of the present Constitution, fixes the order in which the General Assembly shall make appropriations of money, and prohibits any appropriations until that which has precedence in this order has been made. Now the third item in the list is "for free public school purposes." The seventh, and last, is "for the pay of the General Assembly," etc.

In so far, therefore, as the will of the people is expressed in the organic law, the sentiment of Missouri has always been clearly and forcibly stated in behalf of public schools.

There are three other means of testing public sentiment. The attitude of representative citizens, the provisions of the statutes and the character of the schools.

MISSOURI.

The entire sixth article of the Constitution is devoted to providing for common schools, of which there are now about 10,000 in the State, and a "University for the promotion of the arts, literature and science." It should be said, therefore, to the honor of the founders of the Commonwealth of Missouri, that provision for the higher education, as well as for the lower, was no afterthought. It is not something that has been thrust upon the State by any recent measures, but the idea of the district schools and of the University was incorporated into the very life of the State at its birth and now vitalizes its best hopes of the future.

The University contemplated in the formation of the State has been in active operation for about 40 years, and has attained a position, with its faculty of thirty professors, eight hundred students and three-quarters of a million of property, which, at the present, places it in favorable comparison with the leading institutions of the country. When its work and the work of the private schools, academies and colleges are taken into consideration, the opinion may be intelligently and fairly uttered that the people of Missouri have no occasion any longer to send their sons and daughters out of the State to be educated. They can obtain within the State as good an education as they can find without, and will have the additional advantage of growing up with those with whom they will be associated in after life and of strengthening the institutions whose interest they themselves may be expected to share in administering, not to speak of the economy and financial advantages consequent upon patronizing home institutions.

As to the colored people, the State has made a most liberal separate provision for their common schools, and, in Lincoln Institute, for their normal and higher education.

The State sustains four normal schools; including the one for colored students mentioned above, and a normal department of the State University.

The State funds for education (permanent) amount to $8,000,000, and are constantly increasing. In addition to this the State makes special appropriations for the University and normals.

This, in brief outline, is a partial view of education in Missouri, its origin, continuous progress and present excellent condition. In this State the immigrant is assured as substantial guarantees for the education of his children as can be offered anywhere.

LABOR, WAGES AND TAXATION.

IN regard to the laboring classes in Missouri, their privileges, rights and prospects, it can be said that:

The course of legislation in Missouri has wisely tended uniformly toward the protection of the rights of the laborer, so that he has now a lien upon property improved by him, and no property of the employer is exempt from seizure, on execution issued by virtue of a judgment obtained for wages.

The climate of Missouri is such as to allow laborers to work out of doors a very large percentage of the days throughout the whole year, both summer and winter. In the Northern and Eastern States the great depth of snow and extreme cold prevent outdoor labor for four to six months in the year, so that the profits made during the remainder of the year are wholly appropriated to feed the stock of farmers and support families.

72   MISSOURI.

Missouri has not yet made inroads upon her vast natural resources. Her forests are yet to be leveled, her mines developed and worked, her countless acres subdued and cultivated. Again, as she has unprecedented productive power, as varied as great, so she has, by her marvelous transportation facilities, great advantages over States not as fortunately circumstanced, hence her products find ready markets at fair prices, and the industry of man obtains a speedy and adequate reward.

The wages paid in Missouri, regard being had to the time a laborer may work in a year, the cost of living, including food and clothing, compare favorably with wages in other States, and are higher than in a great majority of the States.

SOUTHWEST MISSOURI.

THE great rush of homeless humanity to Oklahoma reveals the important and startling fact that nearly all of the desirable government lands of the United States are already settled and that cheap homesteading, the source of the Nation's rapid growth and prosperity, is nearly at an end. The attention of those now desiring a home on the soil will be drawn to the cheaper improved lands that have been passed over in the rush to occupy the virgin prairies. Among all such regions Missouri, while being the most desirable, has been as well the most neglected and poorly advertised. There are, in this great State, thousands on thousands of acres of great fertility, which could be cultivated and improved at less actual cost than is necessarily involved in a long journey to the Indian Territory.

Southwest Missouri, which includes the counties of Barton, Bates, Cass, Cedar, Cole, Clinton, Johnson, Moniteau, Pettis, Morgan, St. Clair and Vernon, is the most favorably located with respect to desirable farming lands, minerals and numerous other advantages, and offering very cheap lands of any part of the State. These lands will produce a wider range of agricultural and horticultural products than any other equal area in the United States. Where vast mines of coal, zinc, lead, copper, clay, timbered resources and water power are unsurpassed. The climate is the most happy medium between extremes obtainable. The educational facilities are unsurpassed, and a social, moral and religious status is squarely of the highest standard known to the age. At the present the country embraced by the counties named has scarcely more than one-fifth of the population which it is capable of sustaining. Opportunities for manufacturing are unlimited, and lands both improved and unoccupied can be bought remarkably cheap. Now would seem the most opportune time for southwest Missouri. The inevitable reaction from the Oklahoma boom should be made to work to advantage by inviting opportunities for securing cheap homes to the benefit of good and sure markets in this State. A large portion of those who are on the move for the purpose of obtaining a home should have their attention called to the mild and healthful climate of this region. The land, well timbered and well watered with pure limpid streams, numerous medical and mineral springs, where every opportunity is afforded the laborer and capitalist to increase their fortunes and surround themselves with the comforts and luxuries of life. We herewith give a hasty review of the counties just before mentioned.

BARTON COUNTY

Is located in the western tier of counties, about 120 miles south of Kansas City. The surface is gently rolling or undulating, not being too flat to drain well or so rolling as to wash. The soil is a rich, sandy loam, easy of culture and slow to feel the effects of a drought; and, of the 375,000 acres in the county, there is scarcely a quarter section that would not make a desirable farm. The growth of this county has been remarkable. Society is as good as can be found anywhere. In eight years the assessed valuation of the property has increased from $2,000,000 to $5,000,000, and the population more than doubled. There is a permanent school fund of over $124,000 per year; and the great agricultural and fruit products are not alone the source of all her wealth and grandeur. Coal veins of minable thickness are found in over half the townships of the State and the output for the year 1888 approached nearly 200,000 tons. Barton county is in the great fruit valley and possessing innumerable fine orchards, where luscious fruitage finds its way in great quantities to Kansas, Colorado, Texas, Alabama and even Tennessee. This industry demands very little care or expense after once the orchard is planted. There are several thriving towns in the county, containing numerous small manufacturing establishments, and the railroads of the county are amply sufficient for all present needs. Land varies in price, according to location, quality and other considerations that usually give varying values to real estate. Raw lands are worth from $6 to $14 per acre.

WHEAT FIELD, SOUTHWEST MISSOURI. MISSOURI PACIFIC RAILWAY

Improved farms range from $15 to $40, and good farms, with ordinary improvements, can be had from $13 to $25 per acre; and these lands, for agricultural purposes, are not inferior to any in the world.

BATES COUNTY

Is also one of the border counties of Missouri and, in consequence, suffered much during the war and was entirely depopulated. At present it contains a population of 40,000 and assessed valuation of about $8,000,000, which is remarkable considering its condition fifteen years ago. Its rapid development is owing to its unsurpassed natural resources, and the county is entirely free from debt of any nature; has splendid schools and school buildings and a permanent school fund. It is 50 miles south of Kansas City, and the surface in the main is high rolling prairie, with much fine timber. The soil, being for the most part underlaid with limestone, cannot be surpassed in fertility by any county west of the Mississippi. From 40 to 75 bushels per acre of well matured corn is produced each year, and every acre properly cultivated, and the average yield of wheat is from 15 to 30 bushels per acre. Vegetables of all kinds are cultivated with success, and tobacco of fine quality can be grown to advantage. The climate is temperate, the winters short and mild, and, consequently, fruits of all kinds do well. Large orchards of apple and peach trees and fine vineyards of grapes can be found in all parts of the county. Several valuable varieties of hard wood timber are found in the county, including walnut, oak, elm, ash, hickory and linden. It is well watered, having the Osage river and its tributaries, which are fed by perennial springs which abound all over the country. The coal measures underlie the greater part of Bates county, and the number of tons of coal has been estimated at about 6,500,000,000. In addition to coal, there are mines of fine building stones, fire clays, and wells of natural gas have recently been found. Zinc and lead are mined in great quantities at Rich Hill, and this point is rapidly coming into prominence as the manufacturing metropolis of southwest Missouri.

CASS COUNTY

Is another of the border counties of Missouri, a little south of Kansas City, has a large public school fund and school houses furnished with all the latest appliances. All the agricultural products peculiar to this climate, including wheat, corn, oats, barley, flax, millet, orchard grass, timothy and clover, are grown in great profusion and abundance, and is one of the greatest live stock producing counties of the State. There are six railroads crossing the county which have not less than twenty shipping points. Prices of land range from $15 to $100 per acre, governed by quality, location, improvement, etc., which price will be found remarkably low when it is remembered that the northern border of the county is in sight of the smoke of Kansas City. Apples, pears, peaches, apricots, cherries, plums, raspberries and strawberries attain their greatest perfection here.

CEDAR COUNTY

Is in the second tier of counties from the Kansas line; the surface is diversified in the eastern part, being somewhat hilly and broken and covered with timber, while in the western portion it is undulating and principally prairie land. The soil is of two kinds, black loam and red mulatto, grain of all kinds peculiar to this latitude growing luxuriantly. The yield of such products as corn, wheat and oats in favorable years is very high, and of unsurpassed quality. For stock purposes it has as many inducements as any portion of the State. Pasturage is good, water pure and abundant, and many well sheltered localities. This is one of the finest fruit regions in the West. By simply planting the trees, an abundance of apples, plums, cherries, pears, etc., are assured, and small fruits of all kinds seem peculiarly adapted to attain their greatest perfection in Cedar county. The selling price of land ranges from $2.50 to $50 per acre.

There is not a dollar of public indebtedness existing, and taxation is very low. It is well supplied with streams and has abundant water power for manufacturing. Schools receive a large share of public attention; school houses are large and conveniently located and the average term length is seven months. Iron, coal, zinc and lead abound in great quantities, and the mineral springs of Eldorado have already attained great fame as a "health and pleasure resort." No finer timber is found in the State, the quantity is inexhaustible, and consists principally of maple, oak, walnut, hickory and pecan. Here might be established successful furniture and agricultural implement manufactories. The price of timber land ranges from $3 to $8 per acre.

COLE COUNTY

Shares the bounteous gifts which nature has bestowed in southwest Missouri, and its population of late years has been increasing very rapidly. The soil, on account of its limestone basis, is of inexhaustible fertility, easily cultivated and varied in its products. There is abundance of pure water in springs, creeks and rivers, giving it perpetual and abundant supply for flocks and herds, and furnishing excellent drainage over the face of the country. Wheat, rye, corn, barley and oats never fail. Grasses grow in natural and unstinted abundance. All kinds of fruits, vegetables and garden products are of the highest quality, as well as in the greatest abundance. The Missouri washes the northern border and the Osage river flows for nearly 50 miles on the southern and southwestern limits. Of the total area of the county, 240,000 acres, only 70,000 at present are under cultivation, the rest is given over to range and pasture lands. Much of the older land can never be used for any other purpose, but, by careful methods, large quantities of it, ranging in price from $2 to $12, can be brought under successful and profitable cultivation. Churches and schools are well provided in all parts of the county; railroad facilities are unsurpassed, three main lines running into and through the county. Jefferson City, the capital of the State, is located in Cole county. This county is admirably located for dairying and for the raising of sheep and cattle for the markets. There are inexhaustible mines of coal, lead and zinc within the borders of the county.

HENRY COUNTY

Although Missouri was admitted as a State in 1830, it was not until some years after the war that anything of moment was done towards developing this county. It is, properly speaking, a prairie county, amply watered by some 25 streams, whose banks are lined with timber, thus affording abundance of fuel, and that, too, of the best variety, such as black walnut, hickory, pecan, and nearly all the species of oak. The soil is on a limestone base and produces excellent products of almost everything known to this latitude, the staples being corn, wheat, oats and grasses of all kinds. Corn will produce as high as 100 bushels per acre, with good farming, and wheat 40. Fruits do well here and all varieties known to the Temperate Zone are raised, including apples, peaches, plums, apricots, cherries, pears, while grapes and berries are very prolific. Stock raising is a grand success where properly conducted, and

much of the land of this county is specially adapted to this purpose and dairying. Coal is very valuable and large quantities are mined and shipped from the county annually. School and church privileges are well looked after, the county having a permanent school fund of $52,000. Good, fair farming lands can be purchased at from $18 to $25 per acre; the best lands sometimes run as high as $40, although good, well improved places can be had for $25, according to location. These are all improved lands. Cheaper lands can be obtained as low as $15 per acre, and the greater part of the land of the county is capable of being brought under cultivation. Taxes are very low. Considerable attention is given to creameries and dairying, and there is an exceptional opportunity in the county for investment in various manufactories.

JOHNSON COUNTY,

The fairest spot in this wealthy Commonwealth, is situated in the western central part of the State and contains about 900,000 acres, almost every acre of which is tilled. In 1865, Johnson county was sparsely settled, but it now contains a population of 40,000 people, and an assessed valuation of $11,000,000, and all this has been achieved within the short space of 20 years. It is an undulating plain, cut with numerous streams whose banks are covered with heavy belts of valuable timber. The high soil is of rich loam, from two to eight feet in depth, and is underlaid with limestone. The soil produces numerous crops of wheat, corn, barley, rye and oats. Although a prairie country, it is well supplied with timber, consisting of hickory, oak, elm, ash, honey locust, linden and walnut. Grasses grow luxuriantly, and the blue grass springs up spontaneously as in the famous blue grass regions of Kentucky. In addition to its being an excellent farming country, it is also a successful grazing region and is capable of producing the choicest of fruits of all varieties. Coal of the very best quality is found near the surface and natural gas has been discovered. The price of land varies with its quality and location, from $20, $25, $30 and $35 per acre; farms and very choice locations near town sell for $50. These lands have a greater productive capacity than thousands of farms in the older States that sell for $75 and $100 an acre.

MONITEAU COUNTY

Occupies about the exact center of the State of Missouri, is mainly undulating prairie with a deep, black soil, easy to cultivate, and never failing to yield bountiful returns to intelligent cultivation. Corn, wheat, oats, rye, barley, flax and tobacco grow to perfection, as well as all the tame grasses. Stock raising is extensively carried on and constitutes a great source of wealth for those engaged in it. Live stock diseases are almost entirely unknown here. This seems to be the established home of fine fruits. Thousands of bushels of apples are annually shipped from the county, being better than any other crop. Peaches, pears, plums, cherries, apricots and other varieties of small fruits, repay abundantly the labor of the horticulturist. Coal is found near the surface and is extensively mined. Zinc ore is found in great quantities as well as lead, its co-metal. Clays and building stone are also found. The county is well watered, and forests of valuable oak, walnut, hickory, ash and elm cover a large part of the county, affording excellent opportunities for furniture and farming implement manufactories. Schools are amply provided, all the church denominations are represented, and taxes are light. The county is well supplied with railroads, and farming lands can be bought much cheaper here than in less productive lands in other States.

MORGAN COUNTY

Is rich in all the resources of material prosperity. All the grains, fruits and vegetables are abundantly produced. Pasture lands are luxuriant beyond description. This industry is assisted by the numerous springs, streams and rivers of pure water which flow through the county. The county contains about 14,000 population, from all the Eastern and Northern States. They are hospitable, and give a stranger cordial welcome. Immense crops of apples, peaches, pears, cherries and grapes are annually produced. The winters are mild, and cattle are often able to live during the entire winter with little care and attention. The county is well supplied with railroads, public schools, churches, newspapers, etc. Land can be purchased at from $1.50 to $50 per acre. The lower priced land is only adapted to pasturage, but very fine farming lands are obtainable at prices that would astonish an Eastern land buyer.

PETTIS COUNTY

Is one of the central counties of the State, and Sedalia, the county seat, is the largest of the interior towns between St. Louis and Kansas City. There is but little vacant or unimproved land, but the average price of farming lands are lower than the older States, where no better prices for farm produce or shipping facilities prevail. $25 to $40 per acre will purchase the best land in the world, which lies in this county. All kinds of grains, fruits, vegetables, grow in great abundance. Live stock of the finest breeds are reared, and the farms are models of comfort and prosperity. Schools are good, church facilities abundant, taxes low.

VERNON COUNTY,

Out of its 536,000 acres, has not over 25,000 acres of land that cannot be brought under cultivation. The population at present is about 40,000, taxable wealth, $7,500,000. Taxes are low; school districts number 129 in the county outside of the village and city schools; is amply provided with railways, and the best of the land in the county can be obtained from $17 to $40 per acre, as extreme prices. The average price is between $20 and $30; unimproved timber lands at $10 and $12 to $20 per acre. The mineral indications are excellent; coal is found in great abundance, lead and zinc are found in numerous places, and are successfully mined. Iron ore, asphalt, aluminum, mineral paint and potters' clay are also found. The surface of the county is abundantly rolling, while offering excellent drainage. The soil is of a warm nature and of easy cultivation. Wheat and grain raising cannot be excelled; oats, rye and millet also do well. Fruit reaches its greatest perfection, apples, pears, plums, cherries and apricots all being raised successfully, as well as the small fruits. Manufacturing establishments of all kinds are needed, and would be remunerative.

ST. CLAIR COUNTY

Is worthy of the attention of the farmer, capitalist and manufacturer. The surface is made up of fruitful vales and prairies, cut by numerous streams of pure water, and overhung by clear, beautiful skies. The county is well settled, principally by a class of intelligent farmers who till the rich lands with the greatest success, yet good patches of unimproved prairie can be found in various parts of the county that are open for purchase and settlement. There are wooded uplands containing fine timber, consisting of ash, oak, hickory, pecan, etc. Coal, iron, lead and zinc, building stone, paint earths, and many other deposits have been discovered, and there is a chance here for the miner, manufacturer and capitalist, as well as the farmer. Improved farms can be purchased at reasonable figures. Stock raising is extensively engaged in, and the county is well adapted to this and dairying purposes.

SOUTHEAST MISSOURI.

TOPOGRAPHY.

SOUTHEAST Missouri is about nine-tenths hills, mountains, and rolling uplands, and one-tenth bottoms. The Ozark range of hills, sometimes called mountains, extend through the district, from West to East, decreasing in height as they near the Mississippi and spurs of this range and their foot-hills occupy most of the district. The highest peaks and ridges are, generally, covered with a coating of broken chert—a kind of flint, mixed with a red clay loam, of from one to four feet in depth. Amid the highest points are large areas or plateaus of gently rolling clay loam, available for farms and stock ranges. The lower hills are covered with red and yellow clay loam mixed with varying proportions of sand, all extending a depth of four to thirty feet, a strong, fertile soil, easy of cultivation, and very productive. Some of these hill lands contain so large a proportion of sand that they are liable to wash into gullies, when neglected. Underlying a large part of these hills are stratified rocks, principally magnesian limestones, but carboniferous limestone is found in many localities along and near the Mississippi. The whole district gives evidence of volcanic upheaval and at many points granite and porphyry are found in immense masses. The streams run from the Ozarks, to the North, East and South, those running East being mostly small. Piney Fork, of the Gasconade, and the Meramec are lumbering streams, running to the northeast, the last emptying into the Mississippi. Big river, a stream too small for lumbering, is the largest flowing to the East, while to the South run the Whitewater, or Little river, Castor, St. Francois, Black, Little Black, Current, Eleven Point, and the forks of White river. Little river, St. Francois, Black and Current are navigable for steamers from 50 to 150 miles in this State and all the last named streams are largely used for lumbering, as also their tributaries. The entire district is well watered. Springs of limpid water abound in all counties except those of the Mississippi bottom and in those good water is easily obtained by the use of the tube or drive wells.

BOTTOMS.

Each of the rivers mentioned has a bottom of a breadth of from a few hundred feet to miles, and from Commerce, southward to the Arkansas line, extends a bottom, increasing in width, in nearly a triangular outline to about seventy miles wide at the South side, the State line, from East to West. Within this Territory, however, is one range of hills, several miles in width, extending in a southwestern direction, which disappears at the St. Francois river, and reappears in Crawley's ridge, in Arkansas, ending at Helena. The smaller bottoms are generally composed of a clay loam with varying proportions of sand and some streaks of white clay. The broad Mississippi bottom is composed of alternations of low "ridges," usually from two to four feet high and depressions or slashes, a foot or more in depth, the ridges extending in a southerly direction, parallel with the main course of the streams. The ridges are usually from a quarter to half a mile apart. In other words, the surface of the bottom is like a succession of long waves. While the timber remains, the fallen trees dam the flow of the water, causing it to slowly make its way out or to disappear by evaporation. The immense mass of leaves falling from the forest adds to the effect of the tree trunks, in retarding drainage. The average slope or fall of this bottom, to the South, is one to three feet to the mile, so that when the obstructions are removed, the land is at once available for cultivation. The Little, Castor, St. Francois, Black and Little Black rivers cross this bottom, and as their flow is sluggish through the low lands, rubbish accumulates, and during the largest freshets the rivers overflow their banks, generally for a few hours, but the river banks are higher than the lands a mile further back and the spreading waters of the floods find their way back to the rivers miles below the points of escape, and, if retarded by fallen timber the process is slow. These facts caused the name of "swamp lands" to be given to large areas of the finest land in the State which are easily made safe from flood injuries and on which hundreds of excellent farms are now opened. Of actual swamps, but a few thousand acres can be found in Southeast Missouri. The area subject to occasional overflow has been reduced half within a few years, by mill men clearing the rivers of "rafts" and when an inexpensive system of ditching is introduced it will all be tillable. It is as easily drained as were the prairies of Illinois. In every instance, where the clearings have been extended across the slashes, the water has disappeared and the land has become safely tillable. The bottom lands are loose and easy of cultivation and can often be plowed every month in the year.

It should be noted here, that of the lakes marked on the maps, a majority never had an existence and hundreds of thousands of acres so marked were not only never overflowed, but were in fact beautiful prairies, wholly above the highest floods. The name "swamps" attached to these lands by reason of an act of Congress, passed September 28, 1850, donating to the several States all swamp and overflowed lands lying within their boundaries, in trust that the States would severally drain and reclaim them, and after paying the expense of reclamation, convert the remaining proceeds of the sales into the school funds. The cupidity of the States resulted in hundreds of thousands of acres of the best bottom lands and in fact of thousands of acres of hill lands being certified and transferred to the State of Missouri, as swamp and overflowed, which were always safe from overflow. The beautiful prairies of Dunklin county, which are now a succession of the handsomest farms in Missouri, were classed as swamp and overflowed. When the timber is removed, it will be found that there are not 40,000 acres of actual swamp in Southeast Missouri and that all of this can be drained at small expense. It need not be stated that the name "swamp land," has operated greatly to the injury of the district, causing many to avoid it who would have become citizens, had they known the facts. A personal examination will soon satisfy the most skeptical.

SOILS.

There are three kinds of soils to be found in the district, each varying in different localities, but possessing the same general characteristics: the red and yellow clay loam, the white or grey clay, and the brown and dark sandy loam. The first is found throughout the entire hill region, or nine-tenths of the district, and also in many of the smaller valleys and that part of the great bottom near the hills. The color is due to varying proportions of iron oxide or rust. In many places the color is a deep or brick red, while in others it is a light brown, but the fertility is about the same. In most places in the river counties, it contains a good proportion of lime, from the disintegration of the magnesian or other limestone. It is easy to plow, but cannot be safely worked for a day or more after a rain, without risk of forming hard clods. Its fertility, although apparently not as great as that of the sandy bottoms, is practically inexhaustible. Its subsoil is a dense clay and chert or gravel, often almost impervious to moisture, but which contains the elements of fertility. This soil is good for the production of all grains, grasses and vegetables. The winter wheat raised on it is of superior quality and under good cultivation the yield is from 20 to 40 bushels per acre. This soil is also adapted to fruits of all kinds.

The white or grey clay is found in streaks of a hundred or more feet in width and in some localities extends over many acres. It is in no respect equal to the yellow or red clay loam in fertility, is heavy and tends to run together after continued rains. It is not well adapted to vegetables or cotton, but yields fair crops of grass. There is comparatively little of this soil in the district.

The sandy soils are loose, friable and usually have a light and sandy subsoil. They are very fertile, but on the prairies, sometimes become exhausted. In the bottoms, the soil contains more clay and is almost inexhaustible. Many fields that have been cultivated for a quarter of a century show no falling off in crop yields. This land is found throughout the Mississippi bottom. The whole region will, within a few years, become the garden spot of the Mississippi valley. Vegetables of all kinds grow to large size and of excellent quality. For melons, squashes, cotton, corn, it is unexcelled. Corn yields 50 to 100 bushels per acre, cotton half to a bale per acre, potatoes 150 bushels, sweet potatoes 200 bushels, onions 200 to 300 bushels, and other crops in proportion. Grapes do not yield as well as in the hills, being subject to rot, but cherries, apples, plums and peaches bear good crops. Pears will probably yield as well or better in the hills. This soil becomes warm a week or more before the hill land is fit for planting and produces potatoes, radishes, lettuce and other early vegetables from ten to fifteen or twenty days in advance of localities in the same latitude.

MINERALS.

The mineral products of Southeast Missouri are of great variety and immense in quantity. The leading mineral in quantity, as well as in the profit of its mining, is lead. The lead region includes all of Washington, Jefferson, St. Francois and Madison counties and parts of Ste. Genevieve, Perry, Cape Girardeau, Bollinger, Wayne, Iron, Carter, Ripley, Reynolds, Shannon, and probably Stoddard and Butler. The lead formations are of two classes, Galena, which is found in masses of great purity, in holes, called "pockets," or "chimneys," and "disseminated" ore, which, as its name indicates, is scattered in varying degrees of richness through the veins of rock in which it occurs. The veins of this ore are horizontal, or nearly so, like the "blanket" veins of the Leadville district. This ore, before it is smelted, is crushed and "jigged," or washed, by which the lead crystals are separated from the magnesian limestone in which it occurs. In some places, as in the Doe Run mines of St. Francois county, such veins have been found 18 feet thick and in parts of the St. Joe mines, the aggregate thickness of the veins, in a depth of 300 feet, is over 50 feet. The output of the two mines is about one-half of the lead production of the United States, the St. Joe being the largest in the country. Good smelters are well distributed through the district and the daily product is about 4,000 pigs, or nearly 96,000,000 pounds a year. The disseminated lead mines are the best for the laboring men, because the mining, instead of being carried on by men working separately under royalty contracts, is like coal mining, the men being paid regular wages according to the work done. Thriving towns have grown up around each of the larger mines. Next in production, of the mines is iron. This is found in every hill county of the district, but the best mines as yet worked, are in St. Francois, Iron and Crawford counties. The Iron Mountain has yielded millions to its owners and is still as productive as ever, but owing to the present low price of ores, is not worked as vigorously as in the past.

Zinc, in the forms of silicate, dry bone, carbonate and "Black Jack," is found in large deposits, in Jefferson, Washington, St. Francois, Ste. Genevieve and Madison. The zinc mines employ several hundred men and are, as yet, only partially developed.

Manganese is to be found in nearly every hill county of the district, but only a few valuable veins have been opened in Washington, Madison and Iron counties.

Fire clay of quality equal to the famous clays of St. Louis, is in large banks in Ste. Genevieve and Cape Girardeau counties and has been made into bricks. The brick clay of the river counties is also suitable for the best pressed brick and will doubtless be an article of commerce in the near future, as pressed brick is steadily gaining in use in the cities.

Kaolin and China clays are in banks many feet in depth in Jefferson, Ste. Genevieve, Cape Girardeau, Bollinger, Iron and Washington and are believed to underlie a large part of the district.

BUILDING STONES AND MARBLES.

Probably no region of equal area in the United States can show workable quarries of as many useful varieties of building and ornamental stone, as Southeast Missouri. Granite is found in more than a hundred localities and nearly as many shades and colors, from a bright red to a pink, brown, grey, black, green olive, etc. The granites of this district contain little or no mica, will stand an enormous crushing weight, are very hard and withstand atmospheric influences as well as, if not better than, any other American granites. This stone is found in the finest buildings of St. Louis and is steadily gaining in popularity throughout the country. Good building limestone is in half of the counties, the best being in Jefferson, Ste. Genevieve, Cape Girardeau and St. Francois. Marble occurs in at least thirty distinct beds in Madison county, all the strata being variegated and exceedingly beautiful admitting a high polish. The principal colors and shades are pink, mottled, clouded and dotted with white, grey, brown, green, dark red, blue and yellow. The marbles of Ste. Genevieve county are also numerous, found in immense masses and marked in great variety. They are also susceptible of a high polish and are peculiarly adapted for mantels and interior house finish.

Building sandstone of good quality is quarried and in general use in St. Francois, Cape Girardeau, Ste. Genevieve, Perry, Bollinger, Butler, Ripley and Jefferson counties. The best quality is found in inexhaustible strata in Ste. Genevieve, and superior grindstones are furnished by the same quarry.

Porphyry of a quality useful for building purposes, exists in large masses in Iron, Madison, St. Francois and Wayne counties.

CLIMATE.

That the spring comes earlier and the fall ends later, in Southeast Missouri than in States further North, goes without saying; but the differences do not end there. The winters are always mild, the extreme cold being generally about zero (Fahrenheit) and the cold weather with snow and ice lasting less than two months. In occasional winters the temperature has fallen below this, but these are rare. Winter usually begins about the 15th of December, with more rain than snow throughout the season. The coldest weather is generally in January. In February, until the 15th, there are cold days. In the latter part of February there are more warm, spring days than wintry weather. In March, early potatoes are often planted by the 10th and most of the month is available to the farmers to get the ground ready for planting

MISSOURI RIVER, AT BOONVILLE. MISSOURI PACIFIC RAILWAY.

The best farmers plant corn in April and May. Early planting almost invariably pays the best. Cotton is planted in May and June. During the spring months, the weather is generally warm and pleasant. Winter wheat is ready for harvesting from the 20th of June to the 10th of July, the usual time being the 1st of the latter month. Strawberries are in market in April, cherries early in May, peaches from June to November. Concord grapes begin to come into market about the first of August. During the latter part of June, all of July and August, there are many warm days, the thermometer often indicating in the nineties every day for a week or two, but rarely reaching 100 degrees in the shade in any part of the district and then only for a few hours. In the highest hills these extremes of heat are rarely reached. Throughout the district the summer nights are cool and agreeable, ensuring comfortable sleep. The first killing frost rarely occurs before October and heavy frosts but a few days before November. The fall seasons are always delightful, not too warm nor yet too cold for comfort. For consumptives or invalids the climate of Southeast Missouri is very favorable, especially during the fall. In the higher hills the summers, too, are delightful; especially in Iron, Washington and St. Francois counties and parts of Madison, Reynolds, Crawford and Dent. Many visitors spend their summers in these counties and the number increases every year. Were an effort made for such patronage, the mountain portions would be thronged with visitors from the South every summer, on account of the charming scenery and delightful climate.

The vegetable growth of the entire district is rapid and especially in the bottom lands. Pine trees attain a diameter of ten inches in twenty years. Corn often grows 18 feet high. The warm climate, regular rains and fertile soil produce a large return for honest farm labor.

The greatest objection raised to Southeast Missouri has been on the score of health. This has mainly arisen from a misunderstanding of the character of the region. In the first place, nine-tenths of Southeast Missouri is as high above the ocean as Iowa and higher than the average of Illinois or Indiana. The other tenth is bottom land, with far less of actual swamps than were found in Indiana in its settlement. Malarial diseases are not as prevalent in the hill regions of the district as in those of Southern Illinois, or Indiana, in fact no healthier country, on an average, can be found in the United States, east of the Sierras. Consumption, the dreaded spectre of the North and Northeast, very rarely develops in Southeast Missouri, never in bottom regions. Most immigrants, from whatever district they may come, usually find their health improved by residence in the hills of Southeast Missouri. The bottoms are all to the south and southeast, while the summer and fall winds are almost constantly from the west and southwest. The time will come when the mistaken notion of years will be abandoned and the hill regions of this district will be a favorite resort for people of delicate health.

AGRICULTURE.

Although the mineral wealth of the district is great, farming, stock-raising, gardening and fruit culture must, for all time, be the leading industries, employing the largest share of the population. Fortunately the soils are good, the climate favorable, markets are accessible and transportation is cheap. The reorganization of routes of commerce by railroads has given advantages that comparatively few of the older settlers seem to realize, at least thousands have failed to avail themselves of them. Time and the success of those who have been and are up with the times, will even up the condition of farmers and prosperity will be more general.

Grains and grasses thrive well in all parts of the district. The rockiest flint and chert covered hills bear a large annual crop of fine grass, on which thousands of sheep and cattle are fed for months every year, and ten times as many could be well fed. The hill regions, generally, cannot be excelled for clover. The best clover seed in the great markets now comes from the river counties of Southeast Missouri, Cape Girardeau, Scott, Perry, Ste. Genevieve, and the raising of this seed has become a prosperous industry. As stated in the chapters on soils, wheat is the leading crop in all the hill counties bordering on the Mississippi and it also leads in the bottoms of Scott, Mississippi and New Madrid. Under judicious management with this crop the soil improves and the yield also. When one can average twenty bushels per acre, at 70 cents a bushel, on land valued at less than thirty dollars, it is easily seen how much more profitable farming is, than where the same yield of wheat is secured, worth 80 cents a bushel on land valued at $100 an acre. As is well known, with the present mechanical appliances, the cost of cultivating the ground, seeding and harvesting, are about the same in all parts of the country. The yield of oats, barley and rye, are about proportionate to that of wheat throughout the district. Large quantities of oats are raised, but rye and barley are cultivated principally in the northern counties of the district. The Kentucky blue grass thrives as well on the hills of the district as in its native State and is found in all the upland counties. Of the grasses for hay, probably red top does the best and timothy next. In the bottom lands, and especially on the prairies, timothy is liable to "burn out" in the warm weather following haying season and it is sometimes injured in the same way on southern slopes of hills. The average crops of these grasses are not quite as large as in some of the Northern States, but always large enough for a fair profit. Sometimes timothy yields over three tons per acre.

STOCK RAISING

Was, for many years, the main dependence of farmers, as only stock could be driven and transported to market by wagon road and river. In the earlier times, also, there was more dependence placed on the range than now. In those days hogs needed little, if any feeding, more than was necessary to keep them gentle. Now those farmers who keep close watch on their stock and feed often in winter are most successful. There is yet plenty of summer and fall range for cattle in the hills, and the spring range is earlier than in Texas and of excellent quality. Beef cattle can be marketed from the spring range about a month before the Texas beeves come into market, a very desirable feature of the business. In the bottoms, the range for hogs and cattle is good the year round. Sheep and wool have never received the attention deserved. Large ranges well adapted for sheep can be found among the highest hills. Many farmers have found the raising of mules and good horses very profitable and the business may be largely extended without overstocking the market. Poultry raising has become one of the profitable industries in all the counties and with recently improved railroad facilities gains rapidly in volume and steadily in profit. Every hill county contains plenty of tobacco land of the best quality. Tobacco raising was, for years, one of the most profitable industries of the district, but the restrictions of the revenue laws just after the war worked disastrously to thinly settled districts and it was generally abandoned. Doubtless, tobacco will again be a popular crop in the future, as the restrictions are no longer so burdensome and may soon be wholly removed. Dairying has been gaining steadily, in numbers interested, for twenty years in nearly every county, particularly the northern ones. The shipments of milk and cream to St. Louis and Memphis over the St. Louis, Iron Mountain &

Southern railroad have doubled at least twice within the past ten years and are now so large that special milk trains to St. Louis will soon become a necessity. This increase will undoubtedly continue, as hundreds of thousands of acres available for dairy farming and accessible to that road are yet covered with forest. Probably, before many years, there will be found an excellent market for the dairy products of this district in Memphis.

The annual yield of cotton in the district is between 20,000 and 30,000 bales.

Corn is, of course, a staple product everywhere, and it is largely shipped from Scott, Mississippi and Stoddard counties. The bottom land is, generally speaking, the best for corn, although 75 bushels an acre are sometimes raised in the hills. Prices range from 28 to 40 cents.

FRUITS.

No industry is more certain of rapid development and good profits in the district than the raising of fruit. Farmers have known for years that the fruit of Southeast Missouri was at least equal to any raised in neighboring States, but as they found little encouragement from local tradesmen, and local demand was not generally sufficient to warrant going into fruit growing on a large scale, only a few ventured to ship to the markets on commission, and those met with small encouragement. Fruit buyers were of the impression that nothing could be done here and did not visit the district. Last fall there was a strong demand for good apples and buyers were on the alert to find new fields. The exhibit of Southeast Missouri at the St. Louis Exposition included a few samples, from three or four counties, of their fruit products. The buyers were surprised, and on learning that plenty of such fruit could be bought in these counties the dealers sent agents out and within two months had bought more apples from the district than in many years before, and at prices as satisfactory to growers as buyers. This was the beginning of a new era in fruit growing and every year will show a rapid increase in the productions and profits. The dealers last year frankly admitted that in all the territories they visited, within a radius of about 200 miles around St. Louis, they found no fruit surpassing that of this district, either in size, quality or attractiveness of color. They will never overlook the district again. The poorest rocky hills of Southeast Missouri, under reasonable care, will yield large crops of apples, pears, plums, cherries, grapes or other small fruits, and enough peaches can be grown in the district to supply several cities. The profits realized from the only systematically managed orchard in the district, which is also the largest in the State, proved clearly that, acre for acre, fruit growing pays better than any other farm effort and is about equal in profits to most gardens. The fruits that yield the largest profits and lead in quality are, of apples, Ben Davis, Grimes' Golden, Willow-twig, Winesap, and Jonathan; of pears, Bartlet, Seckel and Duchesse D'Angouleme; of plums, any of the best known varieties, and peaches the same. Only the sour or Morello cherries succeed here. The heart cherries do not pay. Of the small fruits, grapes thrive and produce delicious fruit in all the hill regions, also gooseberries, raspberries and blackberries. Currants sometimes pay, but not always. In the average of years, probably apples, pears, grapes and strawberries will be the most profitable of the fruits. Strawberries now yield good returns in Bollinger, Cape Girardeau, Stoddard, Madison, Iron, St. Francois and Butler counties. Direct railway lines to St. Louis, Chicago and Northern cities ensure a constant and increasing market for all small fruits. The western counties of the district have an almost unlimited market for all their fruits in Kansas City, St. Joseph and Northwestern cities and regions. The demand has been so great and the prices so favorable, that no fruit from those counties need be shipped to St. Louis, or is likely to be for many years to come.

TIMBER AND TIMBER PRODUCTS.

Nearly the entire district was covered with forests of pine in the higher hills, and a large variety of timber in the lower hills, valleys and bottoms. The pine is all of the yellow variety, soft and hard, the latter predominating. These pineries yet cover about half a million acres, but are mostly under control of sawmill owners. They daily turn out many hundreds of thousands of feet of superior lumber, most of which is shipped to Northern markets. Oak is in about twenty known varieties, nearly all of great value, and all at least useful. Ash, poplar, gum, elm, walnut, cypress, hickory, tupelo, maple, basswood, catalpa, cottonwood, hackberry, pecan, cherry, beech, box elder, sycamore, ironwood, dogwood, and many other valuable woods grow in great luxuriance. The lumbering interests include investments of millions of dollars in machinery, logs and lands, and will be profitable for many years, as not half of the timber is exhausted. Good oak, gum and hickory lands can be bought at reasonable or even low prices, but they are being rapidly bought by lumbermen and speculators. The best timbered lands now open to purchase are in the bottom counties.

COME AND SEE!!

Words cannot fully describe any country. He who wants a home should not only compare the inducements offered, before making up his mind, but he should finally determine his choice by personal inspection, before a dollar is paid. He should know that the title is good. Some one has the title to each tract and in most cases it can easily be learned by investigation. Speculators can afford to buy doubtful titles, sometimes, but that is not the true policy for farmers. There is plenty of land to be had in every county, at low prices with unquestionable title. The man who will not produce a clear abstract is generally unsafe to deal with. To every one who has read these hints on Southeast Missouri, we give the same advice: Come and See!! Reading is sometimes believing, but seeing is knowing. The visitor will find that the statements above are not overdrawn or misleading. There is no need for misleading any one. This pamphlet is published, not to sell lands, but to induce good people to cast their lot in Missouri. In the course of events this district will be settled, rich and prosperous. We simply wish to hasten the process and realize the advantages of a developed country. It is not mere numbers that are desired, but good neighbors, industrious men. There are many holders of large tracts of land who will sell at reasonable prices and on fair terms. It is cheaper and infinitely better for an industrious man with a few hundred dollars to buy than to rent. A common mistake, however, is buying too much. 160 acres is as much as any farmer with only his family to help and care for, ought to buy, unless he has money to spare to speculate on. A small farm of 80 acres well tilled, will pay better than 160 acres, skinned over.

APPENDIX.

The following statistics, showing, by counties, the commodities marketed by rail, river and express in the State of Missouri during the year 1891, is taken from the official map prepared by Willard C. Hall, Esq., Labor Commissioner.

The abbreviations "c & b" stand for crates and baskets.

ADAIR.

Cattle..........head, 4342
Hogs...........head, 18360
Horses & mules.head, 540
Sheep..........head, 402
Mixed live stock..cars, 11
Wheat........bush, 28074
Corn.........bush, 66284
Oats.........bush, 101989
Mixed grain......cars, 12
Hay............cars, 119
Ties............ties, 84400
Coal............tons, 7614
Shaved hoops....cars, 80
Poultry.......lbs, 208528
Butter.........lbs, 112937
Eggs..........doz, 250170
Other shipments.cars, 160
Small fruit.....c & b, 308

ANDREW.

Cattle..........head, 8140
Hogs...........head, 34860
Horses & mules.head, 800
Sheep..........head, 240
Mixed stock......cars, 2
Wheat........bush, 95788
Corn.........bush, 12180
Other grain......cars, 28
Fruits and vegetables,
              cars, 177
Wood.........cords, 3912
Flour..........bbls, 6000
Poultry........lbs, 75132
Butter.........lbs, 25235
Eggs..........doz, 28740
Cheese.........lbs, 28665
Other shipments.cars, 203
Small fruit....c & b, 1841

ATCHISON.

Cattle........head, 30260
Hogs..........head, 47220
Horses & mules.head, 160
Sheep.........head, 2800
Mixed stock.....cars, 5
Wheat........bush, 129376
Corn.........bush, 677440
Oats.........bush, 18720
Mixed grain......cars, 19
Other shipments..cars, 27
Small fruit....c & b, 2099
Apples.......bbls, 93608
Poultry........lbs, 23200
Butter.........lbs, 6229
Eggs..........doz, 18450

AUDRAIN.

Cattle........head, 12280
Hogs..........head, 46020
Horses and mules,
              head, 5180
Sheep.........head, 12080
Mixed live stock.cars, 115
Wheat........bush, 176648
Corn.........bush, 228520
Oats........bush, 1075360
Mixed grain......cars, 4
Hay............cars, 481
Flax...........cars, 89
Flour.........bbls, 25500
Fire brick......cars, 1064
Lumber.........cars, 90
Coal...........tons, 2790
Lime..........bbls, 24360
Wool..........lbs, 424450
Poultry.......lbs, 765019
Butter........lbs, 68328
Eggs.........doz, 326220
Other shipments.cars, 111
Small fruit.....c & b, 287

BARRY.

Cattle...........head, 220
Hogs...........head, 2340
Horses & mules.head, 140
Sheep..........head, 720
Mixed live stock.cars, 163
Wheat........bush, 183490
Corn.........bush, 40000
Oats..........bush, 8320
Hay............cars, 8
Flour..........bbls, 9450
Ties...........ties, 30400
Cotton.........bales, 230
Potatoes......bbls, 12240
Wood.........cords, 5088
Poultry.......lbs, 110135
Butter.........lbs, 5069
Eggs..........doz, 116790
Other shipments.cars, 315
Small fruit....c & b, 1142
Apples........bbls, 2024
Zinc...........tons, 120

BARTON.

Cattle..........head, 9700
Hogs..........head, 24180
Horses & mules.head,1064
Sheep..........head, 240
Mixed live stock..cars, 25
Wheat........bush, 19282
Corn.........bush, 88750
Oats.........bush, 71760
Hay............cars, 1919
Apples........bbls, 9036
Coal..........tons, 169290
Seed............cars, 63
Poultry........lbs, 90726
Eggs..........doz, 54180
Butter........lbs, 26456
Other shipments.cars, 646
Small fruit...c & b, 22212
Strawberries.....cars, 1
Game..........lbs, 14990

MISSOURI.

BATES.
Cattle..........head, 14720
Hogs..........head, 39780
Horses & mules.head, 903
Sheep..........head, 480
Mixed live stock..cars, 55
Wheat......bush, 188599
Corn......bush, 120667
Oats........bush, 82416
Hay............cars, 293
Flax...........cars, 177
Flour.........bbls, 16200
Apples........bbls, 10175
Coal.......tons, 1031976
Other shipments.cars, 405
Poultry......lbs, 435368
Butter........lbs, 46590
Eggs.........doz, 291690
Small fruit....c & b, 2804
Hides........lbs, 106536
Cheese.......lbs, 43150

BENTON.
Cattle..........head, 3660
Hogs..........head, 38220
Sheep.........head, 1840
Mixed live stock..cars, 46
Wheat......bush, 131924
Corn........bush, 27260
Oats........bush, 31200
Flax............cars, 41
Mixed grain......cars, 4
Lead ore......tons, 80
Ties..........ties, 33800
Wood........cords, 612
Hoops.........cars, 27
Apples.........bbls, 1104
Poultry......lbs, 124234
Butter........lbs, 6860
Eggs..........doz, 120180
Other shipments.cars, 105
Wool.........lbs, 16346
Hides........lbs, 34261

BOLLINGER.
Cattle..........head, 660
Hogs..........head, 1860
Mixed live stock..cars, 25
Sheep.........head, 640
Corn..........bush, 580
Wheat........bush, 31834
Hub lumber.....cars, 10
Ties..........ties, 57400
Staves..........cars, 457
Lumber.........cars, 80
Strawberries....cars, 8
Piling..........cars, 24
Butter.........lbs, 1491
Poultry.......lbs, 92594
Other shipments.cars, 132
Eggs..........doz, 71100
Small fruit....c & b, 6751

Bollinger—Continued.
Wool........lbs, 11677
Dried fruit....lbs, 79117
Hides........lbs, 27213
Logs..........cars, 52

BOONE.
Cattle.........head, 11720
Hogs..........head, 45526
Horses & mules.head, 2183
Sheep.........head, 5937
Mixed live stock..cars, 25
Wheat......bush, 249386
Corn..........bush, 2900
Oats.......bush, 113408
Hay............cars, 15
Flour.........bbls, 14850
Ties.........ties, 41200
Apples.........bbls, 343
Wool.........lbs, 122636
Poultry......lbs, 904284
Butter........lbs, 16536
Eggs.........doz, 374790
Other shipments.cars, 132
Hoop poles.....cars, 71
Feathers......lbs, 3650
Hides........lbs, 29650
Ship stuff.......cars, 4
Clover seed....bush, 576

BUCHANAN.
Cattle.........head, 4063
Hogs..........head, 22650
Horses & mules.head, 580
Sheep.........head, 5920
Wheat......bush, 379420
Corn.......bush, 356720
Oats........bush, 44792
Mixed grain....cars, 178
Flour.........bbls, 42750
Ship stuff.....cars, 217
Fruits and vegetables, cars, 194
Brick..........cars, 1164
Poultry.......lbs, 7460
Butter.......lbs, 107649
Eggs..........doz, 8910
Other shipments.cars,4317
Small fruit...c & b, 14235
Cheese.......lbs, 3630

BUTLER.
Cattle..........head, 80
Hogs..........head, 304
Corn..........bush, 580
Lumber........cars, 983
Ties.........ties, 54000
Staves.........cars, 878
Piling..........cars, 98
Bolts..........cars, 41
Baskets........cars, 17
Eggs..........doz, 6690
Hides........lbs, 49495

Butler—Continued.
Tallow.......lbs, 18120
Ice (6 cars)...lbs, 122245
Small fruit....c & b, 209
Other shipments.cars, 125

CALLAWAY.
Cattle.........head, 4086
Hogs..........head, 18574
Sheep.........head, 6162
Horses & mules.head, 667
Mixed stock......cars, 34
Wheat........bush, 83408
Corn..........bush, 2660
Oats........bush, 34561
Hay............cars, 8
Flour.........bbls, 5550
Fire brick......cars, 532
Ties.........ties, 159600
Lime..........bbls, 28420
Coal...........tons, 558
Apples.........bbls, 485
Poultry......lbs, 314146
Butter........lbs, 1150
Eggs.........doz, 73680
Other shipments..cars, 70
Small fruit....c & b, 432

CALDWELL.
Cattle........head, 14221
Hogs..........head, 50040
Horses & mules.head, 1420
Sheep.........head, 2160
Mixed live stock..cars, 39
Wheat........bush, 55980
Corn.........bush, 44080
Other grains....cars, 12
Apples........bbls, 5365
Oats........bush, 61360
Wool........lbs, 320000
Coal..........tons, 5328
Flour.........bbls, 8700
Poultry......lbs, 406666
Butter........lbs, 93379
Eggs.........doz, 145020
Other shipments.cars, 125
Small fruit....c & b, 447

CAMDEN.
Cattle..........head, 480
Hogs..........head, 1800
Sheep.........head, 400
Mixed live stock..cars, 42
Wheat.........bush, 1244
Oats..........bush, 1040
Lumber.........cars, 16
Apples........bbls, 362
Stone..........cars, 26
Poultry......lbs, 11372
Butter.........lbs, 300
Eggs..........doz, 14070
Game.........lbs, 17657
Dried fruit.....lbs, 1235

COMMODITIES MARKETED 1891.

CAPE GIRARDEAU.

Cattle..........head, 1020
Hogs..........head, 4164
Horses & mules, head, 81
Sheep.........head, 1120
Mixed live stock...cars, 7
Wheat.....bush, 105258
Corn.........bush, 5500
Oats.............bush, 200
Hay..............cars, 11
Flour........bbls, 210000
Lumber.........cars, 188
Staves..........cars, 129
Wood..........cords, 677
Ship stuff.........cars, 26
Poultry........lbs, 267159
Butter..........lbs, 6501
Eggs.........doz, 131670
Ties............ties, 4677
Apples.........bbls, 448
Dried fruit...lbs, 226425
Other shipments, cars, 295

CARROLL.

Cattle.......head, 20868
Hogs.........head, 55140
Horses & mules, head, 530
Sheep..........head, 720
Mixed live stock..cars, 13
Wheat......bush, 1122914
Corn.........bush, 106144
Oats........bush, 48880
Mixed grain......cars, 7
Lumber.........cars, 580
Apples.........bbls, 3686
Flour........bbls, 29100
Ship stuff......cars, 22
Stone.........cars, 145
Tobacco........cars, 18
Poultry......lbs, 238468
Butter.........lbs, 72937
Eggs.........doz, 37470
Other shipments, cars, 136
Small fruit.....c & b, 879

CARTER.

Cattle..........head, 220
Hogs..........head, 240
Oats........bush, 1040
Corn.........bush, 1160
Hay..............cars, 3
Lumber........cars, 3632
Ties..........ties, 12400
Wood..........cords, 60
Other shipments, cars, 18
Poultry........lbs, 250
Eggs..........doz, 300
Hides........lbs, 6600

CASS.

Cattle.........head, 14666
Hogs.........head, 35400
Horses & mules, head, 600
Sheep.........head, 1280
Mixed live stock, cars, 811
Wheat.......bush, 537445
Corn.......bush, 358482
Oats........bush, 116610
Mixed grain......cars, 16
Hay.............cars, 338
Flax.............cars, 93
Apples........bbls, 11100
Brick..........cars, 100
Flour........bbls, 4350
Poultry......lbs, 412902
Butter........lbs, 92648
Eggs.......doz, 177960
Other shipments, cars, 367
Small fruit.....c & b, 549
Game..........lbs, 32944
Hides........lbs, 48249

CHARITON.

Cattle.........head, 9960
Hogs.........head, 34440
Horses & mules, head, 500
Sheep.........head, 800
Mixed stock......cars, 24
Wheat.......bush, 623244
Corn........bush, 59160
Oats........bush, 29120
Tobacco........cars, 118
Canned goods....cars, 15
Flour........bbls, 14850
Ship stuff......cars, 23
Poultry......lbs, 164297
Eggs.........doz, 113520
Other shipments, cars, 178
Small fruit.....c & b, 116
Butter........lbs, 34581
Apples........bbls, 700
Game..........lbs, 7556
Timothy seed..bush, 4797
Fish............lbs, 7033
Hides........lbs, 11525

CHRISTIAN.

Cattle........head, 1000
Hogs.........head, 5220
Horses & mules..head, 20
Sheep.........head, 1680
Mixed live stock, cars, 151
Wheat......bush, 216503
Corn........bush, 16820
Wood........cords, 4932
Ties..........ties, 19000
Cotton........bales, 2521
Lead ore........tons, 90
Poultry......lbs, 700305
Butter.........lbs, 2948
Eggs........doz, 234840
Other shipments, cars, 131
Small fruit....c & b, 3513
Coal props......cars, 112

CLARK.

Cattle.........head, 5503
Hogs.........head, 19763
Horses & mules, head, 564
Sheep.........head, 836
Mixed live stock...cars, 2
Wheat.......bush, 185511
Corn........bush, 319000
Oats........bush, 319173
Mixed grain......cars, 38
Hay.............cars, 176
Rye..........bush, 4372
Timothy seed..bush, 1111
Pickles........cars, 131
Wood..........cords, 1968
Poultry......lbs, 685165
Butter........lbs, 34052
Eggs.........doz, 126030
Hides........lbs, 126490
Potatoes......bbls, 509
Other shipments, cars, 408
Small fruit.....c & b, 327

CLAY.

Cattle.........head, 15222
Hogs.........head, 44681
Horses & mules, head, 2100
Sheep.........head, 4080
Mixed live stock..cars, 33
Wheat......bush, 108278
Corn........bush, 24360
Oats..........bush, 7713
Mixed grain......cars, 51
Flour........bbls, 10500
Brick..........cars, 179
Wood..........cords, 1704
Apples........bbls, 3515
Poultry......lbs, 122076
Axe handles......465923
Butter........lbs, 79463
Eggs.........doz, 90720
Other shipments, cars, 378
Mineral water....cars, 53
Small fruit....c & b, 395
Hides........lbs, 116590
Fish............lbs, 8810
Wool..........lbs, 40122

CLINTON.

Cattle........head, 16300
Hogs.........head, 49087
Horses & mules, head, 1060
Sheep.........head, 2414
Mixed live stock...cars, 4
Wheat.......bush, 8086
Oats........bush, 41642
Corn..........bush, 670
Hay.............cars, 10
Flour........bbls, 7200
Lumber & wood .cars, 575
Poultry......lbs, 226777
Eggs.........doz, 20730
Butter........lbs, 24943
Other shipments, cars, 101
Small fruit....c & b, 1756

MISSOURI.

COLE.

Cattle..........head, 901
Hogs..........head, 10762
Horses & mules..head, 106
Sheep..........head, 777
Mixed live stock..cars, 47
Wheat......bush, 279883
Corn..........bush, 1160
Mixed grain......cars, 2
Flour..........bbls, 72150
Ship stuff......cars, 105
Building brick..cars, 149
Ties..........ties, 307000
Apples........bbls, 370
Wood..........cords, 768
Poultry........lbs, 67475
Tiff............cars, 80
Butter........lbs, 62876
Eggs..........doz, 145350
Other shipments.cars, 122
Small fruit .. c & b, 2931

COOPER.

Cattle..........head, 6637
Hogs..........head, 37923
Horses & mules..head, 633
Sheep..........head, 3200
Mixed live stock..cars, 71
Wheat......bush, 872396
Corn..........bush, 28352
Oats..........bush, 15911
Hay............car, 1
Flour..........bbls, 29850
Ship stuff......cars, 35
Ties..........ties, 20800
Wood..........cords, 2136
Apples........bbls, 2220
Coal..........tons, 396
Poultry........lbs, 217008
Butter........lbs, 15660
Eggs..........doz, 144840
Other shipments.cars, 976
Small fruit....c & b, 165

CRAWFORD.

Cattle..........head, 401
Hogs..........head, 1140
Horses & mules..head, 80
Sheep..........head, 1680
Mixed live stock..cars, 34
Wheat......bush, 123778
Oats..........bush, 1040
Flour..........bbls, 2280
Iron ore......tons, 28314
Pig iron......tons, 15264
Apples........bbls, 2944
Poultry........lbs, 272570
Butter........lbs, 2993
Eggs..........doz, 218580
Other shipments, cars, 169
Small fruit....c & b, 230
Onyx..........cars, 5
Wool..........lbs, 59135

Crawford—Continued.

Hides..........lbs, 82828
Lumber........cars, 8
Ties..........ties, 3200
Dried fruit....lbs, 125000

DADE.

Cattle..........head, 2660
Hogs..........head, 12840
Horses & mules, head, 360
Wheat......bush, 132486
Oats..........bush, 50960
Hay............cars, 164
Apples........bbls, 2775
Lime..........bbls, 85400
Flour..........bbls, 17250
Lead and zinc...tons, 36
Poultry........lbs, 131415
Butter........lbs, 13237
Eggs..........doz, 60630
Other shipments, cars, 197
Game..........lbs, 16505
Small fruit....crates, 55

DAVIESS.

Cattle..........head, 10940
Hogs..........head, 27320
Horses & mules,head, 1203
Sheep..........head, 2320
Mixed live stock, cars, 78
Wheat......bush, 19912
Corn..........bush, 9883
Oats..........bush, 15718
Mixed grain......cars, 7
Wood..........cords, 2604
Apples........bbls, 15725
Flour..........bbls, 8550
Timothy seed, bush, 12888
Poultry........lbs, 925404
Butter........lbs, 47773
Eggs..........doz, 76500
Other shipments, cars, 196
Small fruit....c & b, 59

DENT.

Cattle..........head, 1120
Hogs..........head, 1500
Horses & mules, head, 20
Sheep..........head, 1040
Mixed live stock, cars, 52
Wheat......bush, 94544
Lumber........cars, 109
Apples........bbls, 1656
Iron ore......tons, 4464
Pig iron......tons, 10062
Ties..........ties, 69000
Poultry........lbs, 85275
Eggs..........doz, 51270
Other shipments, cars, 49
Coal..........tons, 324
Charcoal......cars, 20
Junk..........cars, 2
Building brick....cars, 5

DE KALB.

Cattle..........head, 7380
Hogs..........head, 28320
Horses & mules, head, 285
Mixed live stock, cars, 11
Wheat......bush, 7564
Corn..........bush, 67874
Oats..........bush, 26525
Flour..........bbls, 5400
Apples........bbls, 9060
Wood..........cords, 996
Poultry........lbs, 437770
Butter........lbs, 43844
Eggs..........doz, 15180
Other shipments, cars, 326
Small fruit.... c & b, 345

DUNKLIN.

Cattle..........head, 740
Hogs..........head, 1020
Mixed stock......cars, 3
Wheat......bush, 6220
Corn..........bush, 18560
Mixed grain....cars, 164
Flour..........bbls, 300
Cotton........bales, 15433
Cotton seed......cars, 557
Lumber........cars, 959
Staves........cars, 614
Fish..........lbs, 72000
Water melons......cars, 8
Peaches........bask, 60
Poultry........lbs, 9000
Eggs..........doz, 10020
Other shipments, cars, 80
Bacon..........lbs, 2640

FRANKLIN.

Cattle..........head, 6153
Hogs..........head, 15264
Horses & mules, head, 424
Calves........head, 378
Mixed live stock, cars, 315
Sheep..........head, 1754
Wheat......bush, 1183340
Corn..........bush, 94653
Oats..........bush, 3120
Hay............cars, 3
Flour..........bbls, 84000
Wood..........cords, 9492
Ship stuff......cars, 110
Apples........bbls, 7484
Gravel........cars, 1743
Sand..........cars, 748
Poultry........lbs, 613179
Butter........lbs, 205940
Eggs..........doz, 999180
Other shipments, cars, 655
Small fruit.. c & b, 3651

COMMODITIES MARKETED 1891.

GASCONADE.

Cattle..........head, 460
Hogs..........head, 5954
Sheep......head, 333
Mixed live stock..cars, 4
Wheat......bush, 459554
Corn..........bush, 39908
Mixed grain......cars, 6
Flour..........bbls, 21300
Ship stuff........cars, 20
Ties..........ties, 153800
Apples..........bbls, 1531
Wine..............cars, 84
Poultry........lbs, 149789
Butter..........lbs, 17153
Eggs..........doz, 455460
Other shipments..cars, 63
Small fruit....c & b, 3088
Wool..........lbs, 24426
Hides..........lbs, 67338
Tallow..........lbs, 17079

GENTRY.

Cattle..........head, 12444
Hogs..........head, 39180
Horses & mules.head, 450
Sheep..........head, 960
Mixed live stock..cars, 30
Wheat..........bush, 8086
Corn..........bush, 12213
Oats..........bush, 27040
Mixed grain......cars, 1
Apples..........bbls, 8140
Wood..........cords, 4752
Poultry........lbs, 152978
Butter..........lbs, 46986
Eggs..........doz, 36000
Other shipments.cars, 332
Small fruit....c & b, 1624
Wool..........lbs, 7700
Tobacco..........lbs, 1480

GREENE.

Cattle..........head, 4165
Hogs..........head, 17100
Horses & mules.head, 2561
Sheep..........head, 8640
Mixed stock.....cars, 212
Wheat......bush, 236982
Corn..........bush, 58000
Oats..........bush, 37100
Flour..........bbls, 134443
Hay..............cars, 21
Apples..........bbls, 8096
Fruit..........c & b, 12120
Poultry........lbs, 266840
Lime..........bbls, 212660
Butter..........lbs, 12217
Eggs..........doz, 224070
Lumber..........cars, 31

Greene—Continued.

Wood..........cords, 6696
Stone..........cars, 215
Iron ore..........tons, 108
Pig iron..........tons, 18
Cotton..........bales, 851
Lead & zinc....tons, 1314
Other shipments, cars, 1390

GRUNDY.

Cattle..........head, 10610
Hogs..........head, 28800
Horses & mules.head, 440
Sheep..........head, 1840
Mixed live stock...cars, 2
Wheat..........bush, 3110
Corn..........bush, 2350
Oats..........bush, 18720
Mixed grain......cars, 3
Apples..........bbls, 7030
Ties..........ties, 6600
Poultry........lbs, 153058
Butter..........lbs, 15921
Eggs..........doz, 51450
Other shipments.cars, 192
Small fruit....c & b, 1149
Cheese........lbs, 30795

HARRISON.

Cattle..........head, 11360
Hogs..........head, 37440
Sheep..........head, 1260
Wheat..........bush, 1244
Corn..........bush, 107880
Oats..........bush, 95680
Mixed grain......cars, 21
Lumber..........cars, 14
Poultry........lbs, 131183
Butter..........lbs, 5113
Eggs..........doz, 3570
Furs..........lbs, 1476
Meat..........lbs, 1812
Game..........lbs, 325
Raspberries......c & b, 7

HENRY.

Cattle..........head, 18321
Hogs..........head, 40800
Horses & mules.head, 585
Sheep..........head, 1520
Mixed stock.....cars, 377
Wheat......bush, 732100
Corn..........bush, 1380980
Oats..........bush, 264160
Hay............cars, 604
Flax............cars, 142
Flour..........bbls, 100345
Mixed grain......cars, 30
Apples..........bbls, 11952
Fruits..........c & b, 268
Poultry........lbs, 240699

Henry—Continued.

Wool..........lbs, 7995
Eggs..........doz, 332550
Butter..........lbs, 64762
Coal..........tons, 82548
Wood..........cords, 2028
Lumber..........cars, 20
Sewer pipe.....cars, 790
Clay..........cars, 285
Fire brick......cars, 250
Stone..........cars, 62
Other shipments.cars, 642

HOLT.

Cattle..........head, 17660
Hogs..........head, 32880
Horses & mules.head, 1620
Sheep..........head, 880
Wheat..........bush, 186600
Corn..........bush, 348580
Oats..........bush, 7280
Mixed grain......cars, 13
Apples..........bbls, 67340
Rye..........bush, 5236
Wood..........cords, 8712
Canned goods....cars, 29
Poultry........lbs, 515175
Butter..........lbs, 7792
Eggs..........doz, 39540
Other shipments.cars, 251
Small fruit....c & b, 14826

HOWARD.

Cattle..........head, 4071
Hogs..........head, 33702
Horses & mules.head, 545
Sheep..........head, 3600
Mixed live stock..cars, 21
Wheat......bush, 332789
Corn..........bush, 18612
Oats..........bush, 2080
Mixed grain......cars, 1
Flour..........bbls, 51750
Ship stuff........cars, 29
Tobacco........cars, 42
Wood..........cords, 660
Ties..........ties, 2200
Apples..........bbls, 1668
Poultry........lbs, 154680
Butter..........lbs, 15954
Wool..........lbs, 63404
Eggs..........doz, 44070
Other shipments.cars, 175
Small fruit....c & b, 1188

HOWELL.

Cattle..........head, 2320
Hogs..........head, 3300
Horses & mules.head, 920
Wheat......bush, 31722
Corn..........bush, 5800
Oats..........bush, 1040

MISSOURI.

Howell—Continued.
Hay .... cars, 38
Flour .... bbls, 2040
Cotton .... bales, 1150
Lead .... tons, 72
Iron ore .... tons, 2754
Lumber .... cars, 705
Ties .... ties, 43400
Fruit .... cars, 36
Poultry .... lbs, 246044
Eggs .... doz, 190866
Butter .... lbs, 4112
Small fruit ... c & b, 51331
Other shipments. cars, 127

IRON.
Cattle .... head, 1280
Hogs .... head, 1560
Horses & mules .head, 20
Sheep .... head, 320
Mixed stock ..... cars, 2
Wheat .... bush, 1866
Flour .... bbls, 15401
Hay .... car, 1
Poultry .... lbs, 29205
Butter .... lbs, 1838
Eggs .... doz, 46830
Small fruit ..... c & b, 35
Wood .... cords, 576
Apples .... bbls, 185
Lumber .... cars, 2079
Ties .... ties, 22400
Piling .... cars, 317
Granite—building,
  paving, spalls, cars, 1093
Iron ore .... tons, 5706
Other shipments .. cars, 79

JACKSON.
Cattle .... head, 20100
Hogs .... head, 37681
Horses & mules. head, 2865
Sheep .... head, 5419
Mixed stock ..... cars, 50
Wheat .... bush, 317842
Corn .... bush, 68460
Oats .... bush, 31275
Hay .... cars, 119
Flour .... bbls, 124500
Wood .... cords, 2028
Apples .... bbls, 18920
Building brick .. cars, 1758
Paving brick ... cars, 174
Sewer pipe ..... cars, 2380
Poultry .... lbs, 92450
Butter .... lbs, 43840
Eggs .... doz, 57150
Other shipments. cars, 778
Small fruit ... c & b, 2803

JASPER.
Cattle .... head, 2168
Hogs .... head, 9900
Horses & mules. head, 640
Sheep .... head, 80
Mixed stock ..... cars, 16
Wheat .... bush, 261240
Corn .... bush, 12760
Oats .... bush, 14601
Hay .... cars, 250
Flour .... bbls, 252187
Flax .... cars, 46
Ship stuff ...... cars, 129
Building brick .. cars, 123
Wood .... cords, 1848
Apples .... bbls, 4251
Lead & zinc ... tons, 94728
White lead ..... cars, 187
Spelter .... cars, 163
Lime .... bbls, 72520
Other shipments. cars, 2869
Strawberries .... cars, 29
Hides .... lbs, 440000
Poultry .... lbs, 297745
Butter .... lbs, 1521
Eggs .... doz, 28500
Small fruit ... c & b, 13011

JEFFERSON.
Cattle .... head, 4795
Hogs .... head, 4016
Horses & mules. head, 191
Sheep .... head, 415
Calves .... head, 329
Mixed live stock.. cars, 10
Wheat .... bush, 200219
Corn .... bush, 592
Hay .... cars, 22
Wood .... cords, 5784
Flour .... bbls, 8550
Lime .... bbls, 87500
Apples .... bbls, 646
Gravel .... cars, 225
Plate glass ..... cars, 179
Milk .... gals, 482227
Poultry .... lbs, 11989
Butter .... lbs, 2895
Eggs .... doz, 15000
Other shipments. cars, 973
Small fruit ... c & b, 1327

JOHNSON.
Cattle .... head, 15440
Hogs .... head, 54600
Horses & mules. head, 1640
Sheep .... head, 4000
Mixed live stock.. cars, 57
Wheat .... bush, 1255226
Corn .... bush, 885177
Oats .... bush, 203878
Mixed grain ..... cars, 5
Hay .... cars, 136
Flax .... cars, 10

Johnson—Continued.
Flour .... bbls, 25619
Apples .... bbls, 8096
Small fruit ... c & b, 166
Stone .... cars, 515
Coal .... tons, 9648
Clay .... cars, 498
Poultry .... lbs, 261646
Eggs .... doz, 191370
Butter .... lbs, 33178
Wool .... lbs, 26105
Other shipments. cars, 176

KNOX.
Cattle .... head, 5080
Hogs .... head, 18600
Horses & mules. head, 625
Sheep .... head, 1520
Mixed stock ..... cars, 8
Mixed grain ..... cars, 11
Wheat .... bush, 41674
Corn .... bush, 16260
Oats .... bush, 140400
Rye .... bush, 8873
Hay .... cars, 199
Flour .... bbls, 402
Lumber .... cars, 21
Wool .... lbs, 83350
Poultry .... lbs, 93701
Eggs .... doz, 96240
Butter .... lbs, 56467
Small fruit ... c & b, 20
Apples .... bbls, 185
Other shipments. cars, 152

LACLEDE.
Cattle .... head, 1020
Hogs .... head, 4680
Horses & mules. head, 310
Sheep .... head, 1920
Mixed stock .... cars, 155
Wheat .... bush, 173538
Hay .... cars, 15
Flour .... bbls, 6341
Apples .... bbls 6105
Small fruit ... c & b, 12
Lumber .... cars, 20
Wool .... lbs, 7300
Poultry .... lbs, 277474
Butter .... lbs, 2469
Eggs .... doz, 216750
Lead ore .... tons, 20
Other shipments. cars, 43
Wood .... cords, 180
Ties .... ties, 400
Game .... lbs, 61880

LA FAYETTE.
Cattle .... head, 11646
Hogs .... head, 35844
Horses & mules. head, 806
Sheep .... head, 2320
Mixed live stock. cars, 144

COMMODITIES MARKETED 1891. 101

La Fayette—Continued.
Wheat......bush, 1250432
Corn........bush, 478282
Oats........bush, 27270
Hay...............cars, 6
Mixed grain........car, 1
Flour........bbls, 158400
Coal........tons, 454608
Apples........bbls, 9225
Wood........cords, 1428
Meal...........cars, 18
Poultry......lbs, 350406
Butter........lbs, 192566
Eggs.........doz, 224520
Other shipments.cars, 375
Small fruit.....c & b, 439

LAWRENCE.
Cattle..........head, 1440
Hogs..........head, 5580
Horses & mules.head, 140
Sheep.........head, 880
Mixed stock......cars, 56
Wheat......bush, 202472
Corn.........bush, 1753
Oats.........bush, 2080
Flour........bbls, 95079
Lead & zinc...tons, 13620
Poultry.......lbs, 359605
Butter........lbs, 8585
Eggs.........doz, 264600
Small fruit.....c & b, 772
Ship stuff......cars, 113
Sand............cars, 129
Lime.........bbls, 33460
Other shipments..cars, 71

LEWIS.
Cattle..........head, 2967
Hogs..........head, 22311
Horses & mules.head, 922
Sheep.........head, 2968
Wheat......bush, 182484
Corn.........bush, 41162
Oats.........bush, 152854
Hay.............cars, 770
Flour........bbls, 24900
Lumber.........cars, 808
Ties..........ties, 96200
Wood........cords, 2964
Hoops..........cars, 42
Pickles.........cars, 36
Poultry......lbs, 206888
Butter........lbs, 18367
Eggs.........doz, 97860
Wool..........lbs, 63687
Other shipments.cars, 77
Small fruit....c & b, 2200

LINCOLN.
Cattle..........head, 2063
Hogs..........head, 15283
Horses & mules.head, 284
Sheep.........head, 1478

Lincoln—Continued.
Mixed live stock.cars, 283
Wheat......bush, 553732
Corn........bush, 2920
Oats.........bush, 65540
Hay.............cars, 71
Flax............cars, 5
Mixed grain......cars, 7
Lumber........cars, 102
Ties..........ties, 36000
Wood........cords, 612
Apples........bbls, 1117
Poultry......lbs, 517834
Butter........lbs, 10374
Eggs.........doz, 225990
Other shipments.cars, 136
Small fruit....c & b, 2293

LINN.
Cattle.........head, 13280
Hogs.........head, 36120
Horses & mules.head, 500
Sheep.........head, 1600
Wheat.......bush, 54750
Corn.........bush, 5080
Oats.........bush, 50760
Hay.............cars, 106
Mixed grain.....cars, 14
Lumber...........cars, 88
Coal...........tons, 8262
Ties..........ties, 1601
Poultry......lbs, 490070
Butter........lbs, 31157
Eggs.........doz, 21050
Apples........bbls, 5600
Small fruit....c & b, 634
Flour..........bbls, 840
Other shipments.cars, 104
Cooperage......cars, 27
Wood........cords, 276

LIVINGSTON.
Cattle.........head, 5310
Hogs.........head, 31230
Horses & mules.head, 1600
Sheep.........head, 1200
Wheat.......bush, 84607
Corn........bush, 20300
Oats.........bush, 83233
Flour........bbls, 7075
Apples.......bbls, 24472
Small fruit.....c & b, 126
Poultry......lbs, 166089
Butter........lbs, 89476
Eggs.........doz, 508980
Lumber..........cars, 8
Wood........cords, 420
Staves..........cars, 40
Stone...........cars, 160
Wool.........lbs, 175500
Timothy....bush, 11193
Other shipments..cars, 40
Dried apples..lbs, 100000

MACON.
Cattle..........head, 6120
Hogs..........head, 26220
Horses&mules..head, 940
Sheep.........head, 1920
Mixed stock.....cars, 30
Wheat.......bush, 99520
Corn.........bush, 2900
Oats........bush, 27040
Mixed grain......cars, 7
Hay.............cars, 210
Flour.........bbls, 6044
Lumber.........cars, 168
Shaved hoops....cars, 40
Rye.........bush, 2335
Wool.........lbs, 50000
Coal........tons, 404370
Fruit............cars, 33
Other shipments..cars, 55
Poultry......lbs, 1622721
Small fruit.....c & b, 167
Eggs.........doz, 90810
Butter........lbs, 38474

MADISON.
Cattle.........head, 1580
Hogs..........head, 3600
Horses & mules..head, 40
Sheep.........head, 1040
Mixed stock......cars, 3
Wheat.......bush, 21148
Hay.............cars, 10
Flour........bbls, 25022
Lumber.........cars, 746
Ties..........ties, 25000
Charcoal.........cars, 9
Pig lead......tons, 4520
Hoops...........cars, 9
Staves..........cars, 9
Granite.........cars, 51
Poultry......lbs, 252481
Eggs.........doz, 79110
Butter........lbs, 2013
Other shipments..cars, 10
Small fruit.....c & b, 142

MARION.
Cattle.........head, 1983
Hogs..........head, 9688
Horses & mules.head, 558
Sheep.........head, 1652
Wheat.......bush, 84105
Corn.........bush, 5082
Hay.............cars, 27
Flour........bbls, 219000
Lumber.........cars, 6840
Lime........bbls, 223020
Ice............cars, 68
Rip rap........cars, 178
Poultry......lbs, 18978
Butter........lbs, 5179
Eggs.........doz, 8220
Potatoes......bbls, 162

MISSOURI.

Marion—Continued.
Tallow..........lbs, 57896
Hams............lbs, 76070
Bacon...........lbs, 126463
Other shipments.cars, 587
Small fruit.....c & b, 382

McDONALD.
Cattle..........head, 480
Hogs............head, 1980
Sheep...........head, 400
Mixed live stock..cars, 11
Wheat..........bush, 25504
Corn............bush, 2333
Lumber.........cars, 238
Ties............ties, 8400
Wood...........cords, 1956
Props & posts...cars, 382
Small fruit.....c & b, 514
Stone...........cars, 191
Gravel..........cars, 12
Sand............cars, 19
Poultry.........lbs, 32815
Eggs............doz, 25530
Butter..........lbs, 207
Other shipments..cars, 28

MERCER.
Cattle..........head, 5543
Hogs............head, 15480
Horses & mules.head, 260
Sheep...........head, 800
Wheat..........bush, 1244
Corn............bbls, 1160
Oats............bush, 16640
Mixed grain.....cars, 5
Seed............cars, 8
Lumber.........cars, 14
Ties............ties, 8400
Shaved hoops...cars, 3
Stone...........cars, 62
Fruit...........cars, 15
Poultry.........lbs, 146292
Butter..........lbs, 1853
Eggs............doz, 930
Flour...........bbls, 181
Other shipments.cars, 176

MILLER.
Cattle..........head, 960
Hogs............head, 7755
Sheep..........head, 960
Mixed stock.....cars, 37
Wheat..........bush, 37965
Flour...........bbls, 6207
Flax............cars, 2
Lumber.........cars, 2
Ties............ties, 2200
Hoops..........cars, 20
Tiff............cars, 67
Poultry.........lbs, 193350

Miller—Continued.
Butter..........lbs, 4313
Eggs............doz. 52110
Apples..........bbls, 185
Dried fruit.....lbs, 42800
Other shipments..cars, 5
Wool............lbs, 5500

MISSISSIPPI.
Cattle..........head, 1211
Horses & mules..head, 12
Hogs............head, 2817
Wheat..........bush, 119160
Corn............bush, 265788
Mixed grain....cars, 309
Hay.............cars, 11
Vegetables.....cars, 114
Melons..........cars, 707
Flour...........bbls, 27600
Lumber.........cars, 892
Logs............cars, 1072
Poultry.........lbs, 15766
Game...........lbs, 8963
Eggs............doz, 13410
Other shipments..cars, 46
Small fruit.....c & b, 759
Cotton..........bales, 98
Ship stuff......cars, 70

MONITEAU.
Cattle..........head, 2331
Hogs............head, 17461
Horses & mules.head, 660
Sheep...........head, 2169
Mixed live stock.cars, 104
Wheat..........bush, 411883
Corn............bush, 9280
Oats............bush, 50965
Hay.............cars, 9
Flax............car, 1
Apples..........bbls, 3026
Lead ore........tons, 18
Wood...........cords, 1692
Cheese..........lbs, 19946
Wool............lbs, 25265
Hides...........lbs, 49582
Other shipments.cars, 60
Small fruit, c & b, 1220
Poultry.........lbs, 697862
Butter..........lbs, 34822
Eggs............doz, 321030

MONROE.
Cattle..........head, 5944
Hogs............head, 25745
Horses and mules,
               head, 1290
Sheep...........head, 4900
Mixed stock.....cars, 46
Wheat..........bush, 100764
Corn............bush, 580

Monroe—Continued.
Oats............bush, 74880
Mixed grain.....cars, 32
Hay.............cars, 121
Flour...........bbls, 9126
Ship stuff......cars, 18
Lumber.........cars, 38
Ties............ties, 29000
Hoops..........cars, 33
Wood...........cords, 1500
Other shipments..cars, 21
Marble..........car, 1
Wool............lbs, 51032
Stone...........cars, 13
Small fruit.....c & b, 8
Poultry.........lbs, 442278
Eggs............doz, 113340
Butter..........lbs, 8694

MONTGOMERY.
Cattle..........head, 2032
Hogs............head, 19367
Horses & mules.head, 596
Sheep..........head, 1102
Mixed live stock..cars, 35
Wheat..........bush, 114844
Corn............bush, 66120
Oats............bush, 405600
Mixed grain.....car, 1
Flax............cars, 39
Hay.............cars, 20
Ties............ties, 54600
Apples..........bbls, 1005
Poultry.........lbs, 440508
Butter..........lbs, 24987
Coal............tons, 162
Eggs............doz, 167610
Other shipments.cars, 185
Small fruit....c & b, 1220
Wool ....lbs, 11789

MORGAN.
Cattle..........head, 1340
Hogs............head, 10560
Horses & mules.head, 120
Sheep..........head, 560
Mixed stock.....cars, 21
Wheat..........bush, 51626
Oats............bush, 8320
Hay.............car, 1
Flax............cars, 4
Timber.........cars, 10
Ties............ties, 18400
Wood...........cords, 360
Coal............tons, 108
Lead ore and zinc.tons, 60
Canned fruit....cars, 2
Barytes.........tons, 100
Apples..........bbls, 925
Poultry.........lbs, 146974
Game...........lbs, 1965
Eggs............doz, 92250
Butter..........lbs, 35811
Hides...........lbs, 5000
Other shipments...cars, 7

COMMODITIES MARKETED 1891.

NEW MADRID.

Cattle..........head, 404
Hogs ....head, 640
Horses & mules..head, 43
Wheat........bush, 36522
Corn..........bush, 97491
Mixed grain.....cars, 304
Hides..........lbs, 28730
Bacon..........lbs, 54215
Cotton..........lbs, 3083
Cotton seed products,
　　　　　　　lbs, 2500000
Meal ....lbs, 78140
Lumber..........cars, 735
Poultry..........lbs, 7560
Eggs..........doz, 5040
Wool ....lbs, 2671
Castor beans.....lbs, 6400
Tallow.......... lbs, 330
Potatoes........bbls, 33
Cane poles......bdls, 82
Other shipments...cars, 5

NEWTON.

Cattle..........head, 1365
Hogs..........head, 3843
Horses & mules.head, 200
Sheep..........head, 1200
Mixed stock......cars, 34
Wheat...... bush, 215834
Corn..........bush, 1740
Oats..........bush, 1040
Hay..........cars, 41
Mixed grain........car, 1
Flax ....cars, 5
Flour..... ..bbls, 79,690
Lead and zinc..tons, 8820
Wood..........cords, 312
Lumber ....cars, 37
Tripoli ....cars, 53
Lime ....bbls, 2500
Other shipments..cars, 39
Poultry..........lbs, 63476
Apples..........bbls, 2405
Eggs..........doz, 66390
Butter. ... .lbs, 50528
Tobacco ....lbs, 19080

NODAWAY.

Cattle ....head, 31760
Hogs ....head, 81309
Horses & mules.head, 1480
Sheep..........head, 4880
Mixed live stock..cars, 20
Wheat......bush, 138730
Corn......bush, 381110
Oats..........bush, 79270
Rye..........bush, 9340
Flour..........bbls, 2739
Hay..............cars, 7
Mixed grain......cars, 68

Nodaway—Continued.

Lumber..........cars, 31
Wood..........cords, 360
Wool..........lbs, 29000
Potatoes.....bbls, 720
Tile ....cars, 6
Apples........bbls, 67895
Other shipments..cars, 49
Small fruit......c & b, 710
Ice ....cars, 1334
Poultry......lbs, 1546500
Butter.........lbs, 109897
Eggs..........doz, 206850

OREGON.

Cattle..........head, 220
Hogs..........head, 240
Mixed stock......cars, 4
Wheat..........bush, 622
Hay..............car, 1
Lumber..........cars, 3
Posts and piling...cars, 3
Cotton..........bales, 60
Poultry..........lbs, 26980
Eggs..........doz, 45000
Small fruit....c & b, 10425
Other shipments..cars, 17

OSAGE.

Cattle ....head, 869
Hogs ....head, 8094
Horses & mules..head, 74
Mixed live stock..cars, 19
Sheep... ......head, 1122
Wheat......bush, 345966
Corn..........bush, 23214
Oats ....bush, 1042
Flour..........bbls, 9750
Other shipments..cars, 22
Small fruit......c & b, 47
Ties..............ties, 35400
Apples ....bbls, 606
Hoops..........cars, 11
Poultry..........lbs, 117430
Butter..........lbs, 4231
Eggs..........doz, 127770
Wool..........lbs, 4640
Dried fruit.....lbs, 14730

PEMISCOT.

Cattle..........head, 187
Hogs ....head, 333
Horses & mules.. head, 10
Wheat ....bush, 8908
Corn ....bush, 48219
Cotton..........bales, 4116
Cotton seed product,
　　　　　　lbs, 3528133

Pemiscot—Continued.

Fish ....bbls, 732
Pecans ....bush, 739
Hides ....lbs, 18252
Poultry..........lbs, 44245
Eggs..........doz, 5670
Lumber......feet, 1104000
Hay..........bales, 414
Peanuts..........bbls, 201
Wool ....lbs, 1225
Apples..........bbls, 137
Cane poles......bdls, 90
Feathers..........lbs, 292
Other shipments. lbs, 8040

PERRY.

Cattle..........head, 1740
Hogs ....head, 7285
Horses & mules..head, 40
Sheep..........head, 1874
Wheat......bush, 127643
Corn..........bush, 35013
Flour..........bbls, 41473
Lumber..........cars, 11
Apples ... .bbls, 407
Dried fruit....lbs, 433001
Hides.......lbs, 46108
Poultry..........lbs, 234360
Eggs..........doz, 97170
Beans..........lbs, 32091
Butter..........lbs, 4711
Wool..........lbs, 17595
Onions ....bush, 618
Lard ....lbs, 12782
Meat..........lbs, 72526
Other shipments,
　　　　　　lbs, 206866

PETTIS.

Cattle..........head, 14200
Hogs ....head, 32963
Horses and mules,
　　　　　　　head, 1087
Sheep..........head, 6190
Mixed live stock..cars, 62
Wheat......bush, 465426
Corn..........bush, 385760
Oats.. :......bush, 75955
Mixed grain......cars, 2
Hay ....cars, 102
Flax ....cars, 31
Flour..........bbls, 6914
Lumber ....cars, 41
Apples........bbls, 12144
Poultry..........lbs, 291068
Eggs..........doz, 839160
Butter..........lbs, 10752
Small fruit....c & b, 1707
Wool..........lbs, 106600
Other shipments.cars, 154

MISSOURI.

PHELPS.
Cattle..........head, 1780
Hogs...........head, 5280
Horses & mules.head, 560
Sheep..........head, 5040
Mixed live stock.cars, 135
Wheat.......bush, 124400
Corn..........bush, 1162
Oats..........bush, 2100
Hay...............cars, 6
Flour..........bbls, 15900
Apples........bbls, 3214
Iron ore.......tons, 270
Wool........lbs, 444880
Other shipments..cars, 97
Small fruit....c & b, 1114
Ties............ties, 59400
Sand............cars, 325
Poultry......lbs, 450330
Butter.........lbs, 14468
Eggs.........doz, 214980

PIKE.
Cattle........head, 4334
Hogs.........head, 17372
Horses & mules.head, 2327
Sheep.........head, 4556
Mixed live stock.cars, 201
Wheat.......bush, 402434
Oats........bush, 198278
Hay.............cars, 84
Mixed grain.....cars, 11
Flour..........bbls, 39750
Lumber.......cars, 2228
Stone..........cars, 350
Lime........bbls, 95060
Ties..........ties, 23000
Wood........cords. 4140
Wool........lbs, 168961
Poultry......lbs, 392420
Butter.........lbs, 8808
Eggs........doz, 102150
Other shipments.cars, 201
Small fruit....c & b, 5749

PLATTE.
Cattle.........head, 7730
Hogs.........head, 41360
Horses & mules.head, 2496
Sheep..........head, 1680
Mixed stock........car, 1
Wheat.......bush, 283632
Corn........bush, 16820
Mixed grain......cars, 6
Hay.............cars, 33
Flour..........bbls, 25200
Lumber........cars, 311
Apples........bbls, 4416
Wood.........cords, 456
Ship stuff......cars, 28
Lime..........bbls, 7280
Poultry......lbs, 162563
Butter.........lbs, 6074
Eggs.........doz, 60180
Other shipments.cars, 602
Small fruit....c & b, 1393

POLK.
Cattle..........head, 3100
Hogs..........head, 19560
Horses & mules.head, 1120
Sheep..........head, 4960
Mixed live stock...cars 72
Wheat........bush, 57846
Corn..........bush, 74240
Oats..........bush, 30160
Hay.............cars, 41
Mixed grain......cars, 3
Apples.........bbls, 2410
Wood........cords, 2712
Charcoal........cars, 179
Poultry........lbs, 475640
Butter.........lbs, 21999
Eggs.........doz, 152070
Other shipments.cars, 255
Small fruit......c & b, 251
Dried fruit....lbs, 27676

PULASKI.
Cattle..........head, 980
Hogs...........head, 7320
Horses & mules..head, 80
Sheep..........head, 2320
Mixed live stock.cars, 165
Wheat.......bush, 149280
Corn..........bush, 580
Hay.............cars, 2
Ties..........ties, 15200
Apples.........bbls, 1560
Onyx............car, 1
Dried fruit....lbs, 116526
Other shipments..cars, 37
Game..........lbs, 20975
Poultry......lbs, 131306
Butter.........lbs, 2986
Eggs.........doz, 202410
Hides.........lbs, 27301
Wool..........lbs, 11340

PUTNAM.
Cattle..........head, 6060
Hogs..........head, 12000
Horses & mules.head, 760
Sheep..........head, 480
Mixed live stock...cars, 3
Wheat........bush, 2488
Corn..........bush, 9860
Oats..........lbs, 28080
Mixed grain......cars, 4
Apples.........bbls, 4297
Hoops..........cars, 23
Timothy seed..bush, 1080
Coal.........tons, 72540
Poultry......lbs, 130823
Butter........lbs, 60703
Eggs.........doz, 200730
Hides.........lbs, 32640
Other shipments...cars, 5
Small fruit......c & b, 13

RALLS.
Cattle..........head, 1200
Hogs...........head, 7980
Horses & mules..head, 40
Sheep..........head, 1120
Mixed live stock..cars, 19
Wheat.......bush, 216456
Corn..........bush, 616
Oats..........bush, 15600
Hay.............cars, 35
Brick...........cars, 2
Lumber.........cars, 14
Ties............ties, 2600
Wood.........cords, 1140
Logs............cars, 4
Poultry......lbs, 15860
Butter.........lbs, 1315
Eggs.........doz, 5520
Wool..........lbs, 8170
Broom corn....lbs, 9630
Small fruit......boxes, 5

RANDOLPH.
Cattle..........head, 5450
Hogs..........head, 18846
Horses and mules,
              head, 1370
Sheep..........head, 6800
Mixed live stock..cars, 37
Wheat........bush, 87080
Corn..........bush, 580
Oats..........bush, 12480
Flour..........bbls, 31500
Coal........tons, 176274
Brick..........cars, 313
Ties..........ties, 41200
Hoops..........cars, 42
Hay.............cars, 73
Eggs.........doz, 90390
Game..........lbs, 5428
Other shipments.cars, 145
Small fruit.....c & b, 497
Poultry......lbs, 148442
Butter.........lbs, 3269

RAY.
Cattle.........head, 11880
Hogs.........head, 33253
Horses & mules.head, 200
Sheep..........head, 640
Mixed live stock..cars, 36
Wheat.......bush, 341097
Oats.........bush, 13550
Corn........bush, 53170
Other grain.....cars, 4
Hay.............cars, 12
Lumber........cars, 364
Coal........tons, 195048
Wood.........cords, 768
Poultry......lbs, 201148
Butter........lbs, 11004

COMMODITIES MARKETED 1891.

R.iy—Continued.
Eggs..........doz, 66360
Small fruit.....c & b, 194
Other shipments.cars, 135
Flour..........bbls, 6150
Apples..........bbls, 555

REYNOLDS.
Lumber.........cars, 271
Ties............ties, 2400

RIPLEY.
Cattle..........head, 440
Hogs..........head, 3000
Sheep.........head, 160
Mixed live stock...cars, 2
Lumber.........cars, 366
Ties............ties, 33600
Cotton.......bales, 1110
Timber.........cars, 65
Shaved hoops.....cars, 21
Staves.........cars, 133
Poultry........lbs, 158240
Eggs..........doz, 33210
Dried fruit.....lbs, 12000
Hides..........lbs, 2371
Potatoes........bbls, 79
Other shipments..cars, 80

SALINE.
Cattle........head, 29534
Hogs.........head, 59426
Horses and mules, head, 2802
Sheep.........head, 4889
Mixed stock......cars, 61
Wheat......bush, 1008041
Corn.........bush, 436148
Oats.........bush, 21742
Mixed grain.......cars, 7
Hay...........cars, 17
Hemp straw......cars, 18
Wood.........cords, 2844
Ship stuff.......cars, 151
Flour..........bbls, 87600
Wool..........lbs, 304905
Apples.........bbls, 1656
Poultry........lbs, 305260
Butter.........lbs, 9128
Eggs..........doz, 63180
Other shipments.cars, 209
Small fruit......c & b, 84

SCHUYLER.
Cattle.........head, 6000
Hogs.........head, 27120
Horses and mules, head, 1200
Sheep........head, 3520

Schuyler—Continued.
Mixed live stock...cars, 2
Wheat........bush, 31722
Corn.........bush, 60332
Oats.........bush, 76311
Mixed grain......cars, 8
Hay.............cars, 7
Ties............ties, 27600
Wood..........cords, 768
Hoops..........cars, 31
Apples.........bbls, 2000
Wool..........lbs, 240000
Poultry........lbs, 261413
Butter.........lbs, 141318
Eggs..........doz, 183870
Other shipments.cars, 103
Small fruit.....c & b, 694

SCOTLAND.
Cattle.........head, 3980
Hogs.........head, 17760
Horses and mules, head, 1340
Sheep.........head, 880
Wheat........bush, 3648
Corn.........bush, 12760
Oats.........bush, 131041
Mixed grain......cars, 9
Hay............cars, 3
Wood..........cords, 288
Timothy seed..bush, 2887
Ties............ties, 9000
Cooperage......cars, 16
Poultry........lbs, 489660
Butter.........lbs, 95662
Eggs..........doz, 182580
Other shipments.cars, 124
Small fruit......c & b, 21
Wool..........lbs, 14300

SCOTT.
Cattle.........head, 777
Hogs.........head, 2699
Horses & mules..head, 12
Sheep.........head, 13
Mixed stock......cars, 4
Wheat........bush, 283654
Corn.........bush, 418230
Hay............cars, 2
Flour..........bbls, 40050
Water melons..cars, 1006
Cantaloupes.....cars, 40
Lumber.........cars, 428
Bran...........bbls, 7254
Wool..........lbs, 5537
Hides..........lbs, 17858
Ship stuff......cars, 21
Poultry........lbs, 32471
Butter.........lbs, 421
Eggs..........doz, 24390
Small fruit....c & b, 2168
Other shipments..cars, 56

SHANNON.
Cattle..........head, 60
Mixed live stock...cars, 8
Corn.........bush, 3480
Lumber.........cars, 4900
Ties............ties, 2260
Hay............cars, 3
Ties and piling...cars, 41
Logs...........cars, 1625
Wood..........cords, 12
Poultry........lbs, 700
Eggs..........doz, 480
Game..........lbs, 1621
Other shipments..cars, 63

SHELBY.
Cattle.........head, 6040
Hogs.........head, 27660
Horses & mules.head, 1160
Sheep..... ...head, 5360
Mixed live stock....car, 1
Wheat........bush, 149280
Corn.........bush, 76560
Oats.........bush, 112320
Mixed grain......cars, 9
Hay...........cars, 324
Hoops.........cars, 74
Wool..........lbs, 40000
Poultry........lbs, 164221
Butter.........lbs, 2556
Eggs..........doz, 4380
Apples.........bbls, 600
Other shipments..cars, 49

ST. CHARLES.
Cattle.........head, 2224
Hogs.........head, 15194
Horses & mules.head, 403
Sheep.........head, 1355
Mixed live stock.cars, 105
Wheat........bush, 827109
Corn.........bush, 104583
Oats.........bush, 38899
Mixed grain......cars, 11
Hay............cars, 9
Flour..........bbls, 54600
Apples.........bbls, 20761
Ties............ties, 28129
Stone..........cars, 1030
Onions.......bush, 84456
Wood..........cords, 1344
Small fruit....c & b, 13033
Poultry........lbs, 459082
Butter.........lbs, 70457
Hides..........lbs, 188393
Eggs..........doz, 454560
Other shipments.cars, 779

ST. CLAIR.
Cattle.........head, 4240
Hogs.........head, 16260
Horses & mules.head, 100
Sheep.......head, 400

MISSOURI.

St. Clair—Continued.
Mixed live stock.cars, 245
Wheat........bush, 22392
Corn........bush, 390340
Oats........bush, 36400
Hay...........cars, 292
Flax...........cars, 42
Ties..........ties, 10800
Apples........bbls, 7560
Wood.........cords, 372
Gravel........cars, 435
Poultry.......lbs, 264830
Butter........lbs, 7241
Eggs.........doz, 145110
Cheese........lbs, 34390
Other shipments.cars, 217
Small fruit....c & b, 153

STE. GENEVIEVE.
Cattle..........head, 797
Hogs..........head, 4584
Horses & mules, head, 47
Sheep.........head, 1166
Wheat........bush, 89186
Corn.........bush, 2804
Oats.........bush, 238
Flour.........bbls, 46998
Apples........bbls, 693
Onions........bbls, 1469
Dried fruit....lbs, 284632
Hides.........lbs, 89459
Wool..........lbs, 24278
Poultry.......lbs, 316963
Eggs.........doz, 181680
Butter........lbs, 8052
Lumber........cars, 14
Lime ....bbls, 11147
Beans.........lbs, 39091
Bran..........bbls, 8283
Other shipments,
            lbs, 407551

ST. FRANCOIS.
Cattle.........head, 1740
Hogs..........head, 2040
Horses & mules, head, 120
Sheep.........head, 1120
Mixed live stock, cars, 30
Wheat........bush, 18666
Corn.........bush, 6960
Oats.........bush, 6409
Hay...........cars, 17
Mixed grain.....cars, 7
Flour.........bbls, 30600
Pig lead......tons, 18594
Iron ore......tons, 56628
Zinc..........tons, 1026
Granite.......cars, 808
Paving blocks...cars, 502
Poultry.......lbs, 44841
Butter........lbs, 9368
Eggs.........doz, 38400
Other shipments,cars, 588
Small fruit....c & b, 132

ST. LOUIS.
Cattle..........head, 4768
Hogs..........head, 4722
Horses & mules, head, 178
Sheep.........head, 583
Mixed live stock...cars, 7
Wheat........bush, 789781
Corn........bush, 10515
Mixed grain......car, 1
Hay...........cars, 7
Stone.........cars, 1279
Sand..........cars, 1654
Building brick..cars, 1340
Fire brick.....cars, 9329
Tile..........cars, 2211
Lime.........bbls, 38080
Poultry.......lbs, 17262
Butter........lbs, 4781
Eggs.........doz, 15900
Other shipments, cars,1690
Small fruit....c & b, 4259
Wood.........cords, 6384

STODDARD.
Cattle.........head, 602
Hogs..........head, 8070
Wheat........bush, 18051
Corn.........bush, 64987
Oats.........bush, 1070
Mixed grain.....cars, 86
Flour.........bbls, 20700
Cotton seed....cars, 41
Lumber........cars, 1648
Ties..........ties, 187200
Cotton........bales, 945
Hay............cars, 2
Staves........cars, 493
Logs..........cars, 115
Granite........cars, 86
Wood.........cords, 1800
Poultry.......lbs, 149390
Butter........lbs, 590
Eggs.........doz, 109530
Other shipments.cars, 162
Small fruit....c & b, 625

SULLIVAN.
Cattle.........head, 16060
Hogs..........head, 20220
Horses & mules,
            head, 1030
Sheep.........head, 1680
Mixed live stock...cars, 6
Wheat........bush, 16903
Corn.........bush, 1208
Oats.........bush, 12480
Mixed grain.....cars, 8
Hay...........cars, 12
Timothy seed..bush, 1814
Ties..........ties, 38000
Apples........bbls, 3388
Wood.........cords, 2268
Coal..........tons, 630

Sullivan—Continued.
Hoops..........cars, 43
Poultry.......lbs, 353233
Butter........lbs, 67593
Eggs.........doz, 153210
Other shipments..cars, 79
Wool..........lbs, 54164

TEXAS.
Cattle.........head, 160
Hogs..........head, 600
Mixed live stock...cars, 2
Wheat........bush, 3732
Hay............car, 1
Ship stuff.....cars, 2
Sand............car, 1
Lumber........cars, 180
Posts & piling....cars, 739
Apples........bbls, 750
Poultry.......lbs, 31920
Butter........lbs, 4310
Eggs.........doz, 10290
Peaches......baskets, 163
Feathers......lbs, 895
Other shipments, cars, 15

VERNON.
Cattle.........head, 9900
Hogs..........head, 17940
Horses & mules.head, 860
Sheep.........head, 320
Mixed live stock..cars, 63
Wheat........bush, 36010
Corn.........bush, 104306
Oats.........bush, 89442
Hay...........cars, 793
Flax..........cars, 181
Mixed grain.....cars, 9
Apples........bbls, 19545
Castor beans....cars, 62
Coal..........tons, 33408
Clay..........cars, 239
Poultry.......lbs, 747760
Butter........lbs, 28054
Eggs.........doz, 257820
Other shipments.cars, 741
Small fruit...c & b, 27194
Strawberries....cars, 2

WAYNE.
Cattle.........head, 1200
Hogs..........head, 1592
Horses & mules..head, 20
Wheat........bush, 3110
Corn.........bush, 1170
Hay...........cars, 22
Mixed live stock...cars, 9
Lumber ....cars, 2918
Ties..........ties, 310400
Staves........cars, 350

COMMODITIES MARKETED 1891.

Wayne—Continued.
Stone............cars, 467
Piling.......... cars, 162
Crushed granite..cars, 45
Granite spalls....cars, 60
Poultry.........lbs, 52855
Butter...........lbs, 135
Eggs...........doz 30510
Game.............lbs, 9865
Other shipments..cars, 21
Small fruit......c & b, 342
Hides...........lbs, 11505

WEBSTER.
Cattle..........head, 2120
Hogs ....head, 5520
Horses & mules.head, 280
Sheep......... head, 2560
Mixed live stock..cars, 17
Wheat.......bush, 105118
Corn...........bush, 1740
Oats...........bush, 1040
Hay ....cars, 9
Apples.........bbls, 3471
Posts & piling...cars, 549
Lumber..........cars, 70
Wool ....lbs, 40000
Dried fruit .....lbs, 80160
Poultry.......lbs, 709885
Butter...........lbs, 2030
Eggs..........doz, 166380
Game............lbs, 75838
Other shipments.cars, 632
Small fruit......c & b, 393
Hides..........lbs, 25000

WARREN.
Cattle..........head, 588
Hogs..........head, 2657
Horses & mules..head 22

Warren—Continued.
Sheep..........head, 665
Mixed live stock..cars, 34
Wheat.......bush, 106228
Corn ....bush, 16874
Oats..........bush, 35360
Mixed grain........car, 1
Flax..............cars, 4
Ties............ties, 82600
Apples..........bbls, 994
Wood........cords, 1152
Clay..... ....cars, 209
Poultry....... lbs, 218502
Butter..........lbs, 20535
Eggs........doz, 293850
Other shipments.cars, 173
Small fruit....c & b, 6523
Dried fruit....lbs, 20860

WASHINGTON.
Cattle..........head, 920
Hogs ....head, 2640
Horses & mules.head, 210
Sheep..........head, 640
Mixed live stock....car, 1
Wheat........bush, 11843
Corn.........bush, 17980
Oats..........bush, 1040
Hay ....cars, 7
Zinc ore........tons, 72
Pig lead.......tons, 1260
Lead ore.........tons, 90
Tiff.............cars, 371
Wood........cords, 6732
Poultry.........lbs, 65469
Butter..........lbs, 26239
Eggs.......... doz, 45180
Milk ....galls, 5938
Other shipments..cars, 31
Small fruit......c & b, 135
Charcoal..........cars, 86

WORTH.
Cattle.........head, 4700
Hogs..........head, 18900
Sheep...........head, 80
Mixed live stock....car, 1
Wheat.........bush, 4354
Corn.........bush, 32480
Oats..........bush, 6240
Mixed grain......cars, 38
Apples.........bbls, 5935
Wool...........lbs, 20000
Poultry........lbs, 10425
Butter..........lbs, 8053
Eggs.......... doz, 36330
Other shipments..cars, 19
Small fruit......c & b, 57

WRIGHT.
Cattle..........head, 1340
Hogs.......... head, 6960
Mixed live stock..cars, 38
Wheat........bush, 48516
Corn.........bush, 8120
Hay ....cars, 4
Ship stuff... .....cars, 32
Lumber ....cars, 37
Posts & piling...cars, 736
Fruit............cars, 15
Cotton.........bales, 46
Poultry.......lbs, 431220
Butter.........lbs, 21568
Eggs..........doz, 168060
Game...........lbs, 44495
Fresh meat......lbs, 68920
Small fruit....c & b, 6192
Other shipments.cars, 170
Furs..........lbs, 1135
Coke..............car, 1

SUMMARY.

Counties			Quantity	Unit	Commodity
105	Counties	Marketed	629,438	head	Cattle.
105	"	"	2,006,444	"	Hogs.
88	"	"	65,927	"	Horses and Mules.
90	"	"	190,631	"	Sheep.
104	"	"	28,049,177	pounds	Poultry.
105	"	"	14,090,426	dozen	Eggs.
87	"	"	5,415	cars	Mixed Live Stock.
101	"	"	21,635,458	bushels	Wheat.
92	"	"	9,652,938	"	Corn.
76	"	"	5,152,701	"	Oats.
67	"	"	8,284	cars	Hay.
53	"	"	1,617	"	Mixed Grain.
62	"	"	2,295,746	barrels	Flour.
19	"	"	1,155	cars	Shipstuff.
69	"	"	544,914	barrels	Apples.
95	"	"	2,949,537	pounds	Butter.
86	"	"	264,720	baskets	and crates Small Fruit.
51	"	"	119,873	cords	Wood.
52	"	"	34,445	cars	Lumber.
22	"	"	2,152	"	Hoops.
47	"	"	2,314,806		Ties.
40	"	"	3,135,685	pounds	Wool.
7	"	"	35,770	bushels	Timothy Seed.
15	"	"	321,007	pounds	Game.
4	"	"	88,625	"	Fish.
26	"	"	1,689,994	"	Hides.
3	"	"	72	cars	Seed.
17	"	"	7,250	"	Stone.
13	"	"	921,407	barrels	Lime.
6	"	"	160,576	pounds	Cheese.
14	"	"	1,564,162	"	Dried Fruit.
2	"	"	2,611	"	Furs.
6	"	"	402,643	"	Meat.
5	"	"	30,156	bushels	Rye.
6	"	"	13,743	barrels	Potatoes.
4	"	"	5,387	cars	Sewer Pipe and Tile.
13	"	"	16,482	"	Brick.
3	"	"	1,408	"	Ice.
20	"	"	2,655,882	tons	Coal.
17	"	"	862	cars	Flax.
3	"	"	89,481	bushels	Onions.
3	"	"	178	cars	Tobacco.
3	"	"	46	"	Canned Goods.
15	"	"	144,540	tons	Lead and Zinc.
7	"	"	123,571	"	Iron.
12	"	"	29,652	bales	Cotton.
4	"	"	23,763,133	pounds	Cotton Seed Products.
2	"	"	1,761	cars	Melons.
103	"	"	46,779	"	Other Shipments.

COMMODITIES MARKETED 1891. 109

Value of Surplus Commodities.

Commodity.	Quantity.	Value.	Total Value.
Cattle, by rail	621,840 head		
" " river	7,598 "		
Total	629,438 head at	$ 40 00,	$25,177,520
Hogs, by rail	1,973,174 head		
" " river	33,270 "		
Total	2,006,444 head at	8 00,	16,051,552
Horses and Mules, by rail	64,405 head		
" " " " river	1,522 "		
Total	65,927 head at	100 00,	6,592,700
Sheep, by rail	184,973 head		
" " river	5,658 "		
Total	190,631 head at	4 00,	762,524
Wheat, by rail	20,275,475 bush.		
" " river	1,359,983 "		
Total	21,635,458 bush. at	80,	17,308,366
Corn, by rail	9,257,514 bush.		
" " river	395,524 "		
Total	9,652,938 bush. at	35,	3,378,528
Oats, by rail	5,127,675 bush.		
" " river	25,026 "		
Total	5,152,701 bush. at	25,	1,288,175
Wool, by rail	3,112,519 lbs.		
" " river	123,166 "		
Total	3,235,685 lbs. at	20,	647,137
Poultry, by rail	27,143,009 lbs.		
" " river	906,168 "		
Total	28,049,177 lbs. at	10,	2,804,918
Butter, by rail	2,928,055 lbs.		
" " river	21,482 "		
Total	2,949,537 lbs. at	15,	442,431
Eggs, by rail	13,437,806 doz.		
" " river	652,620 "		
Total	14,090,426 doz. at	10,	1,409,043
Ties, by rail	2,307,487 ties		
" " river	7,319 "		
Total	2,314,806 ties at	30,	694,442
Dried Fruit, by rail	879,505 lbs.		
" " river	684,657 "		
Total	1,564,162 lbs. at	04,	62,566

MISSOURI.

COMMODITY.	QUANTITY.	VALUE.	TOTAL VALUE.
Flour, by rail	2,190,983 bbls.		
" " river	104,763 "		
Total	2,295,746 bbls. at	$ 3 50,	$ 8,035,111
Apples by rail	540,953 bbls.		
" " river	3,961 "		
Total	544,914 bbls. at	1 75,	953,599
Mixed Live Stock, by rail	5,415 cars at	500 00,	2,707,500
Hay, by rail and river	8,284 " "	260 00,	2,153,840
Wood, by rail	119,873 cords "	3 00,	359,619
Lumber, by rail and river	34,445 cars "	185 00,	6,372,325
Hoops, by rail and river	2,152 " "	190 00,	408,880
Timothy Seed, by rail	35,770 bush "	1 27,	45,428
Game, by rail	321,007 lbs. "	20,	64,201
Fish, by rail and river	88,625 " "	05,	4,431
Hides, by rail and river	1,689,994 " "	05,	84,500
Stone, by rail	7,250 cars "	125 00,	906,250
Lime, by rail and river	921,407 bbls "	52,	479,132
Cheese, by rail	160,576 lbs. "	06,	9,635
Rye, by rail	30,156 bush "	75,	22,617
Potatoes, by rail and river	13,743 bbls. "	96,	13,193
Sewer Pipe and Tile, by rail	5,387 cars "	195 00,	1,050,465
Brick, by rail	16,482 " "	73 68,	1,214,394
Ice, by rail	1,408 " "	61 50,	86,592
Coal, by rail	2,655,882 tons "	1 31¼,	3,488,058
Lead and Zinc, by rail	144,540 " "	32 80,	4,740,912
Iron, by rail	123,571 " "	2 39,	295,335
Flax, by rail	862 cars "	400 00,	344,800
Onions, by rail and river	89,481 bush "	80,	71,585
Tobacco, by rail	178 cars "	1,008 00,	179,424
Canned Goods, by rail	46 " "	650 00,	29,900
Cotton, by rail and river	29,652 bales "	35 00,	1,037,820
Cotton Seed Products by rail and river	23,763,133 lbs. "	7 00,	88,167
Melons, by rail	1,761 cars "	75 00,	132,075
Grass Seed, by rail	72 " "	1,260 00,	90,720
Meat, by rail and river	402,643 lbs. "	10,	40,264
Ship stuff, by rail and river	1,155 cars "	240 00,	277,200
Mixed Grain, by rail	1,617 " "	343 00,	554,631
Other Shipments, by rail and river	46,779 " "	250 00,	11,694,750
Small Fruit, by rail and river	264,720 c & b "	1 50,	397,080

Value of Total Shipments, - $125,049,335

COMPARATIVE STATEMENT.

Lead and Zinc	$4,740,300
Corn and Oats	4,666,703
Poultry, Butter and Eggs	4,656,392
Coal and Iron	3,783,393
Sewer Pipe, Brick and Tile	2,264,859

Iron Mountain Route.

4 —DAILY TRAINS— 4

—TO THE—

SOUTHWEST

—EQUIPPED WITH—

Pullman Buffet Sleeping Cars,

Free Reclining Chair Cars,

and Elegant Day Coaches.

—ALL POINTS IN—

Southeast Missouri,

—AND TO—

MEMPHIS, LITTLE ROCK, HOUSTON, GALVESTON, AUSTIN, SAN ANTONIO. LAREDO (where Direct Connection is made for the CITY OF MEXICO), DALLAS, FORT WORTH, EL PASO, LOS ANGELES and SAN FRANCISCO.

THE COLORADO SHORT LINE

MISSOURI PACIFIC RY.

SOLID TRAINS, EQUIPPED WITH

FREE RECLINING CHAIR CARS

——AND——

PULLMAN BUFFET SLEEPING CARS,

LEAVE **ST. LOUIS** DAILY

——AND RUN——

THROUGH VIA KANSAS CITY,

——TO——

PUEBLO AND *DENVER*

WITHOUT CHANGE,

WHERE CONNECTIONS ARE MADE FOR

ALL ROCKY MOUNTAIN POINTS.

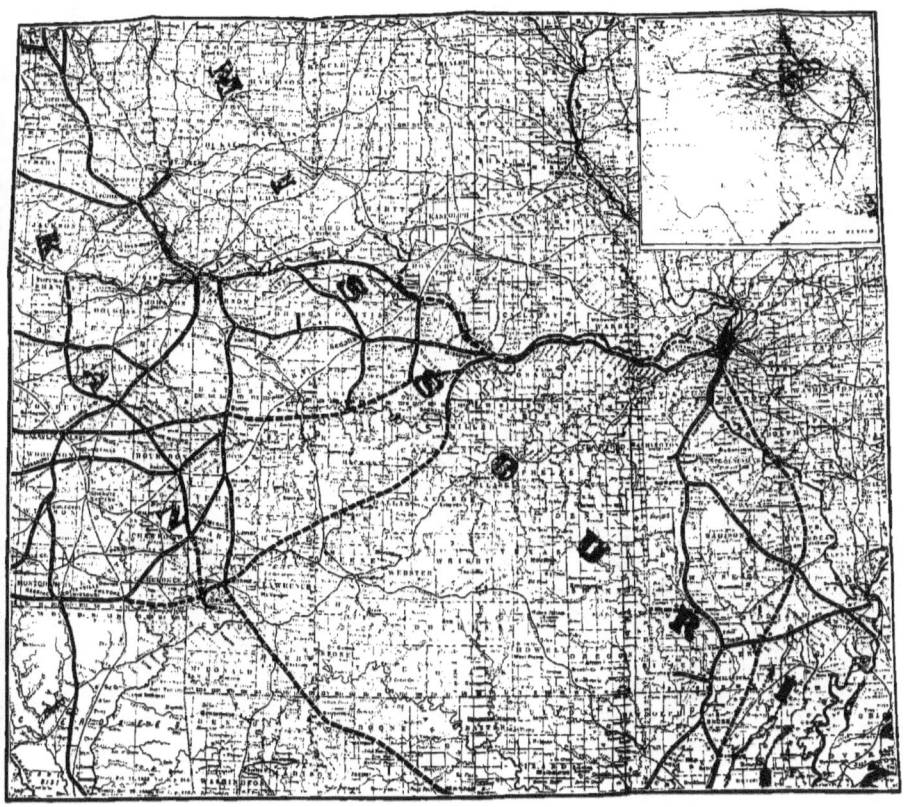

www.ingramcontent.com/pod-product-compliance
Lightning Source LLC
Chambersburg PA
CBHW030405170426
43202CB00010B/1493